A SAILING

TO THE

Solent and Poole Harbour

*WITH PRACTICAL HINTS
AS TO LIVING AND COOKING ON AND
WORKING A SMALL YACHT*

BY

LIEUT.-COLONEL T. G. CUTHELL

WITH FOUR CHARTS.

Contents.

CHAPTER I.

INTRODUCTION 1

CHAPTER II.

COOKING, CATERING, ETC.

A Small Yacht—The Waterproof Cover—Bedding—What to Take—Cooking Lamps—Utensils—The Culinary Art—A Six Days' *Menu*—Hints and Recipes . . . 6

CHAPTER III.

UP PORTSMOUTH HARBOUR.

Sailing Directions — Portsmouth — To Fareham — Sailing Directions—Titchfield —To Porchester — Sailing Directions—To Southwick and Boarhunt 16

CHAPTER IV.

TO LANGSTON, HAYLING, AND UP CHICHESTER HARBOUR.

Sailing Directions—Hayling Island—Up Chichester Harbour—Sailing Directions—Thorney Island—Emsworth—Warblington — To Bosham — Sailing Directions — Bosham Church—To Chichester— Sailing Directions — Chichester Cathedral — Chichester — Goodwood — West Hampnett—Boxgrove 22

CONTENTS.

CHAPTER V.
To Bembridge and Brading Harbour.

Sailing Directions—Bembridge—Whitecliff Bay—Yaverland—Brading—Roman Villa—Nunwell—Invasions . . 35

CHAPTER VI.
To Seaview, Ryde, Wootton Creek, and Cowes.

Sailing Directions — St. Helen's — Seaview—Ryde — Quarr Abbey — Wootton Creek—Sailing Directions—King's Quay—Osborne—East Cowes—Whippingham . . . 40

CHAPTER VII.
Up the Medina.

Sailing Directions—West Cowes—Newport—Carrisbrooke . 47

CHAPTER VIII.
To Newtown.

Sailing Directions—Gurnard—Newtown—Admiral "Snip"—Shalfleet—Mottistone—Swainston 50

CHAPTER IX.
To Yarmouth.

Sailing Directions—Yarmouth—Freshwater—Farringford—Freshwater to Alum Bay 53

CHAPTER X.
Round and about the Needles.

Sailing Directions—Totland Bay—Sailing Directions—Alum Bay—The Needles—Scratchell's Bay—Freshwater Cliffs 57

CHAPTER XI.
To Swanage.

Sailing Directions — Swanage —Tilly Whim — St. Alban's Head 60

CONTENTS. vii

CHAPTER XII.

To Studland.

Sailing Directions—Studland—Ballard Down—The Agglestone Rock 64

CHAPTER XIII.

Up Poole Harbour.

Sailing Directions—Poole Harbour—Branksea Island—Poole — Wimborne — Wareham — Bindon Abbey — Lulworth Castle—Lulworth Cove—Corfe Castle 67

CHAPTER XIV.

To Bournemouth, Christchurch, Hurst, and Lymington.

Sailing Directions—Bournemouth — Christchurch — Sailing Directions — Hurst Castle — Lymington — Boldre — Brockenhurst 80

CHAPTER XV.

Up Beaulieu River.

Sailing Directions—Beaulieu River—Lepe—Buckler's Hard—Beaulieu Abbey 85

CHAPTER XVI.

Up Southampton Water.

Sailing Directions—Fawley—Eaglehurst—Calshot Castle—Eling — Southampton — Bitterne — Netley Abbey — Hamble—Titchfield River—Lee-on-the-Solent . . . 91

CHAPTER I.

Introduction.

THIS little book is intended to enhance the pleasure of those who go down to the sea in ships during the summer months cruising, in their temporary floating houses, along the beautiful southern shores of our island. Many yachtsmen, other than enthusiastic racing men, grow weary of day after day at sea, and like to combine the pleasure of yachting with that of sight-seeing on shore, done comfortably from their own movable hotel. Land guide-books merely treat of the country as accessible by road or rail. But when lying in harbour the yachtsman often finds himself, without being aware of it, close to objects of interest which he would have journeyed far to see if he had been on land. Our island is so rich in beautiful scenery, especially near the coast, so teeming with interesting remains, with history written in stones, with "ancestral homes" and stately fanes, which we are all too apt to ignore and neglect because they are not in a foreign land.

It is hoped that this guide will prove useful to the experienced yachtsman, the owner of a large vessel, for he will find in it much information respecting places of interest up creeks and rivers, which, though too shallow for his yacht, are yet accessible to his steam launch and gig.

But it is for the increasing class of owners of small yachts and sailing boats of ten tons and under that this book is especially intended. It will open up to them inlets and rivers of smooth and safe water, which will indeed call forth all their skill in navigation, and tax all their judgment, but which will well reward their exertions by the "fresh fields and pastures new" along their shores.

This increasing class of amateurs consists, generally, of amateurs unaided by paid hands, of men out for a cruise of it may be days, it may be weeks, intent on living a joyous, untrammelled, healthy picnic life in flannels, doing their own sailing, and cooking and cleaning. What the delights of such a life are, only those who have tried it can realize!

In endeavouring to unite the pleasures, therefore, of camping out and sailing in waters less circumscribed and monotonous than those of a river, the Solent naturally suggests itself as the most suitable place on our coasts. No waters are so sheltered, or offer so much variety both in estuaries and in coast scenery. The Americans affirm it to be the best sailing ground in the world; neither so shallow as their own, nor so deep as the Scotch, affording an anchorage everywhere afloat. This guide has therefore been arranged for a cruise beginning and ending at Portsmouth, as the nearest starting point to London. But it can be taken up at any point where a yacht can lie, and can be made to cover weeks or only days. Eastwards we have gone as far as Chichester Harbour, which, though open to the English Channel, can be easily reached by coasting round from Portsmouth. To the west we have taken in Bournemouth Bay, Swanage Bay, and Poole Harbour, though these lie beyond the limits of the Solent.

For they can be reached from thence through the Needles passage, or taken as centres for separate cruises, Swanage Bay opening up the Isle of Purbeck, a little-known corner of our S.W. coast, and Poole Harbour being a paradise for small yachts, where many days can be well spent.

With a view to the camping-out element in a cruise in a small boat we have added a chapter on what to take on board, and also a six days' *menu* of three good wholesome meals a day, which can be concocted over a spirit lamp by the most inexperienced cook.

This is not intended to be a text-book on sailing. It pre-supposes that the amateur has had some experience and knows how to sail his boat. But we have appended a few practical hints on the navigating of tidal waters and on getting on and off moorings, which are the result of practical experience and will prove useful. Rather is our intention to supplement the English Channel Pilot Book, which should lie on every cabin table, but which does not enter into details concerning the shallow tidal waters where small craft can penetrate. For practical instruction in the art of sailing we refer the yachtsman to Mr. E. F. Knight's book on "Sailing" in Bell's All England Series, a handy little compendious volume, which may be studied with advantage.

In the Sailing Directions which head each chapter no directions have been given as to lights. The Pilot Book supplies all such information. But in this book no night sailing is contemplated. The cruises are intentionally short, for it adds immensely to the pleasure, comfort, and safety of amateur yachting if an early start is made in the morning, and the vessel on her anchorage with everything snug well before dark.

It has often been said that the two greatest difficulties for amateurs in working yachts are—first, to get away from your anchor; and secondly, to take up moorings. This is certainly the case with the Solent. The strong tide running under one, the narrowness of the channel, and the number of vessels about one in harbour, all add to the difficulty.

In getting away, all these things must be considered— how the tide is running? how strong it is? how much sail should be set? how the wind is blowing? from what quarter?

In a narrow river it is often necessary to swing on your moorings by means of a rope, to set your jib and to run out to sea, setting the rest of your sail as you go out. But if you are on your own anchor, of necessity you must get it on board, and then bring the yacht sharp round. Sometimes the tide is running in, and the wind blowing in also. It is then necessary to set all your sail, and do the best you can to stem the force of the elements, often to no purpose. When, on the other hand, the wind is blowing out and the tide running out too, and you have all sail set and want to get out, it is advantageous to run up the river a few yards and then gybe round to get clear of the other vessels, and thus come round in as short a space as possible.

In taking up moorings it is best, if possible, to avoid scandalizing your mainsail or jib, and for this reason. If you miss the moorings, and your anchor is not ready to let go at once, you are not so likely, under certain conditions of wind and tide, to take the ground. If it suits, shorten sail, if you will, but always bring the vessel's head to wind over the moorings, with very little way left on her, if possible. Even a lady can manage this, with practice, by keeping away from the wind and making a graceful sweep round up to the mark; and a very pretty manœuvre it is when well executed.

In tacking up a river an excellent rule is never to sail beyond the ripple, if there is any tide under you. Avoid smooth water; that way mud lies.

In the Solent, when befogged in a small yacht, the first thing is to get up the compass, and, setting it in position, carefully to take your bearings. Next hold on to them until you come close in shore; hug the shore as long as you can make it out with sufficient water under you. Then, when the shore blots out, let go your anchor. You will find yourself then in a position too near in shore to be in any danger from passing steamers, and you will also know whereabouts you are.

CHAPTER II.

Cooking, Catering, etc.

A YACHT of about five tons, drawing four feet six or thereabouts, can get into most of the rivers and all the harbours in the Solent at half-tide. A vessel this size will make up three berths and give a very good-sized cockpit to steer from, which will hold comfortably five people. Every one can keep dry except the man at the helm, who is comfortably wrapped up in his oilys. Ladies, as a rule, prefer the open air. But there are moments when they would rather keep out of the rain; therefore a cabin, however small, is an advantage to shelter in. A boat such as we are describing, and suitable for the ensuing trips, is emphatically a day boat. The intention is to be up and off early, and to get into port again before four in the afternoon. If the cabin has a raised roof and a sliding hatchway, there will be about five feet head room when the hatch is closed. A waterproof sheet to cover this raised deck at night, or in case of rain, is much to be recommended. It is fastened to the coaming of the deck by ties and eyelet holes. For, do what you will, the sun and the wind always open the seams of a raised deck, and to have a drip of water descend on to one's bed in the night is, to say the least of it, objectionable. The cabin doors should be left open summer and winter, to keep the vessel dry and clean. The waterproof cover over the cockpit keeps all rain out.

In the following pages we imagine that a party of amateurs are cruising alone without any paid or professional yacht's hand. It means doing everything for oneself without the inconvenience of having to provide room, food, and conversation for a sailor, not to mention the thirty shillings a week wages he demands. Both order, method, and cleanliness should be the rule of the boat. The cabin, when more than two are on board, should be devoted to sleeping and clothes, books and papers; only the lockers in the well to sails, gear, wine, food, oil, lamps, etc. The beds should be made up after breakfast, and the cabin tidied up.

It is everything to sleep warm and dry, even in summer weather. Sheets and pillow-cases are essential; three sheets and two pillow-cases, a fur rug, and two blankets, for each bed. If the berths are merely wooden bunks, a thin but good horse-hair mattress, the right size to fit them, *i.e.* about two feet wide, is a necessity. But in a vessel the size I am describing, there is room in the bows for a canvas bed on an iron frame to fold up against the side in the day-time.

How often in any form of camping out, when a paid hand is not employed, dirty plates, untidy beds, smoky lamps, uncoiled ropes, etc., are the order of the day. A place for everything, and everything in its place, should be the motto of every yacht, large or small.

A folding table upon which to eat in the cabin, and which can be stowed when sailing, is a comfort. The cooking, such as I am going later to describe, can all be done with a swinging lamp, hung before the mast and fed with spirits of wine. Oil stoves in a small and lively boat are unmanageable, dirty, and smelly.

When starting for a cruise of some days or even a

week or two duration, the lockers in the well should contain the following items:—Biscuit-tins for bread; potatoes; tea and sugar; onions; tomatoes; rice; soda for washing up; can of oil for the riding-light; biscuits; bacon; eggs; fowls; meat; fish; wine, beer, or spirits; spirits of wine; soap; cotton waste for cleaning purposes; bath-brick to clean the brasses and knives; salad oil; salad dressing; vinegar; sauces; pepper and salt; tins of jam; figs; prunes; tins of corned beef; soups; green vegetables, such as French beans, etc.; besides plates, cups and saucers; a tea-strainer; wire sieve; strainer; two saucepans; omelette pan; knives, spoons, and forks. An extra spirit-lamp, to stand, will be useful for more elaborate cookery. A false bottom, on three legs an inch high, of perforated block-tin, is a useful addition to one of the saucepans. On this we can finish off a dish. On this we can steam fish or potatoes, and lift them out dry.

Use as few plates, etc., as possible, but wash up after every meal, keeping some very hot water, a small dish-brush, and some soda for the purpose.

Is it Voltaire who said: "Le superflu, chose très-nécessaire"? It is not the quantity of things one takes which goes to make one comfortable. Quite the reverse. But it is the presence of the *chose très-nécessaire*: the corkscrew; the tooth-brush; the nail-scissors; the knife; the hammer; the gimlet; the stamps; the egg-cups; matches; razor; soap; the sponge; hair-brush; looking-glass; handkerchiefs; socks; collars; house-wife, with needle and thread and button; the towels; the dish-cloth; the map of the country; the prayer-book; cookery book; bottle of vaseline; packet of plaster; all these small things that take up no room in a boat, that need never be shifted, but that go far towards making a cruise comfortable.

Atkey, of Cowes, has a patent swinging spirit-lamp to be recommended. It holds a tin kettle large enough to boil seven breakfast-cups full of water, and on to it fits a saucepan and frying-pan—the former with the strainer above described. An extra lamp and boiler, which does not swing, is useful in harbour. Both lamps burn spirits of wine—a gallon of which should last about a fortnight. Both lamps have three burners, but except for the purpose of boiling water for tea, or for frying a chop, or boiling water for potatoes, but one is used at a time.

China cups and saucers are best; those in metal burn the mouth. Plates should be of enamel iron. Three cups and saucers; three tumblers; three egg-cups; three sets of soup, meat, and cheese-plates in a set are enough. The water-can should hold five gallons, and have a false bottom and a tap, and be taken ashore to be re-filled daily. A tea-strainer is useful when making tea for a large party, as the kettle can then be used to make the tea in.

Hooks and a rack ranged round the bulk-head of the cabin should hold the cups, tumblers, and any glass bottles.

Except when moored close along shore in a dirty harbour, the day should begin with a dip overboard. In the evening, about tea-time, the same performance* is very refreshing. An early start advisable; and even if it is made at five a.m., a cup of tea and a rusk or biscuit should be served out all round previously. Keep to regular hours as much as possible, and let your hour for turning in depend on how hard the day has been.

On a coasting cruise like the one we are imagining, it

is necessary and possible to go ashore every day for supplies; one of the crew doing the marketing while the others are tidying and cleaning up the boat. We therefore append a *menu* for six days, with simple recipes for cooking each dish with the lamps and utensils above described, and ensuring a complete variety of wholesome, fresh food. People are too apt to imagine that because they have no culinary experience, it is necessary, when camping out in a boat or in a tent, to live on provisions of the tin-tin-ny.

First Day.

Buy three French rolls, a large sole, a quart of milk, six eggs, 1 lb. fresh butter ; a crusty loaf, a cake, a 7-lbs. tin of toast biscuits ; a leg of mutton, a bunch of carrots and turnips. Tea, coffee, sugar, onions, and potatoes are already in store.

Cook the sole in sea-water. Tie a bit of thread to its head ; when the sea-water boils, put the sole into the saucepan. In about six or seven minutes prod it with a fork. If the meat adheres to the bone, it is not sufficiently cooked. Directly the meat comes away it is done. Pour away the water, and serve the fish on a dish, cut in three. Coffee or tea and milk ; French rolls ; butter ; jam ; and three eggs, is the breakfast.

For lunch, cut the leg of mutton in half, and cut off it some three large pieces. Place these in some cold water, with a little salt, over the spirit-lamp. When it begins to boil, skim well all the scum off the pot. Let it boil in water enough to cover it, slowly, on a low lamp for an hour. Then add potatoes, carrots, onions, a little Worcester sauce, and pepper, and let it boil for another hour. Then serve, and with bread, butter, and cheese, you will have a capital mid-day meal.

· At night open a tin of beef; one of ox-tail soup; some preserved prunes, and coffee.

Second Day.

When ashore next day buy one pound of plums, two mackerel, three French rolls, some milk, bread, and six eggs.

For breakfast, put the eggs into a dish and beat up with some milk. Add a couple of rashers of bacon, cut up into dice, and one spring onion cut up fine, some pepper and salt, and a few drops of Worcestershire sauce. Light the lamp; butter a frying-pan, and pour the above mixture into it. As it cooks, keep turning the mixture with a fork, to prevent its adhering to the frying-pan, in which serve it. Cold beef, biscuits and marmalade complete the breakfast.

For lunch, fry in butter some of the leg of mutton with salt, adding a spring onion.

At night boil some potatoes; cut off the heads of the mackerel, and cut their bodies in two. To boil potatoes, after washing and paring them (two to each person), place them in sea-water, which will begin to boil in about twenty minutes, and the potatoes will take about twenty minutes longer, but should be tested with a fork, to see if they are soft. The water should then be nearly all poured away. On this occasion the fish are to be put into the saucepan, and the lid put on, ten minutes after the potatoes have been boiling. If the flame is good, in about fifteen minutes' time the fish and potatoes will be ready to serve; but the fork should again be brought into requisition to test it, for a raw fish is uneatable.

Some time during the day boil some rice, enough for three times. Put about a pennyworth of rice into a saucepan of water, large enough to drown it in, having washed it well first in clean water. When the water boils, throw it all away and put in some more. When this boils, after about ten minutes, inspect the rice, which should be soft to the touch; then turn it all out into the sieve, and throw cold water on it. At night, serve some of this cold rice, which has been drying all day in the sieve, with plums. These should have their stalks pulled off, and be placed in a syrup made of a tumbler of water and quarter pound of white sugar, and be allowed to cook for about fifteen minutes till quite soft, and then put away to get cold for use.

Third Day.

Buy a fowl, milk, butter (one pound), two lemons, some currants, a small tin of curry powder, two vegetable marrows, rolls and bread, a piece of salmon, middle cut, about one pound, two lettuces.

For breakfast, tie the salmon up in a sheet of clean writing-paper, with cotton, and place it in the frying-pan with a large piece of butter. Let it fry slowly, say twenty minutes, till done.

For lunch, mutton fried, cake, lettuce salad.

At night, cut up the chicken and curry it, after frying it in butter in the frying-pan (*vide* receipt at end of chapter). Heat some rice by putting it into a saucepan with the lid on, with about one inch of hot water, the rice to rest on the strainer aforementioned.

Fourth Day.

Buy butter, milk, steak (three pounds); sardines and fish (three pounds); three mild bloaters; a fowl; six eggs ;

a jam roll from a pastry-cook's, a pint of cream, one pound flour; one pound shin of beef; a cake.

For breakfast, fry the bloaters in clean note-paper, in butter; three eggs, boil three minutes; jam, biscuits, French rolls, and coffee and cream.

For lunch : Immediately after breakfast fry the steak in butter. Place it in saucepan with a pint of water and a teaspoonful of flour, some walnut ketchup, and all the butter it was fried in. Fry onions in butter and add. Add potatoes, carrots cut in slices, a piece of sugar, and half a glass of claret. Allow to simmer on fire for four hours. This will be excellent heated up next day with fresh boiled potatoes.

At night, boil the codfish, till tender, for say twenty minutes; remove with strainer from the saucepan. Jam roll and cheese make up the meal.

Fifth Day.

This is provided for by the stores laid in on the preceding day, in order to show how to manage when unable to go ashore, or not within reach of shops. We suppose there is bread enough left, and some cream.

The codfish, with some of the rice, some butter, two hard-boiled eggs, pepper and salt, must be mashed up together and heated in a frying-pan, and served *very* hot.

For lunch, boil the fowl for half an hour in water enough to half cover it ; then add the rest of the cream, six tomatoes (from stores), three onions, five potatoes, salt, and keep the corner of the saucepan on for one hour more.

At night, a tin of soup, some "spotted dick" pudding, made with quarter-pound suet, finely chopped, a handful of currants nicely cleaned, a cupful of milk, a tablespoonful of sugar, three eggs, three-quarters pound of flour, all nicely mixed, and put into a floured cloth, tied up, and boiled for three hours. This will fry up excellently in a frying-pan with a little butter and pounded sugar.

Sixth Day.

For meat ring some of the above changes of fry; stew and boil. Put the rest of the rice into a cup of milk, which has had beaten into it in a saucepan two eggs, with a tablespoonful of white sugar and a little lemon juice. Boil for ten minutes and leave to get cold. Cut up, pare and core some apples, and boil for ten minutes in a syrup of sugar and water, and put away to eat cold with the rice.

Macaroni may be boiled in water for thirty-five minutes; then the water poured off, a tablespoonful of butter, and two tablespoonfuls of grated Parmesan cheese added, and the whole kept on the lamp for six or seven minutes, and not allowed to burn. In place of cheese three sliced tomatoes may be put in.

A good rule in camp cooking is always to look ahead and boil more than you want. What is left will always fry up. Extra potatoes can always be fried up.

Always fry fish in one frying-pan in butter, and meat in another frying-pan in butter. The same butter will do again for the fish, or the same butter for the meat, but they must not be mixed. When you have used your frying-pan, pour any butter in it into a clean jam-pot for future use.

The following two easy dishes will make a change:—

Vegetable Marrow Soup.—Boil a young vegetable marrow till quite tender, then pass through wire sieve. Put into saucepan with a pint of milk, a piece of salt, pepper, a large piece of butter; makes nice soup in about twenty minutes.

Curry should be made of white meat. Either of boiled cod or of veal or chicken; when uncooked, fry first. Take salt, curry powder or paste, rice, two lemons, a breakfast cup full of milk, a few peas, vegetable marrow, quarter-pound of butter, some onions. Boil the milk for half an hour. Add the curry powder, a tablespoonful. Fry the onions in half the butter, and add to saucepan. Fry the meat or fish, cut in small pieces in the rest of the butter, and add to the saucepan. Add a little salt. Fill a wineglass with lemon juice, and pour into saucepan. Boil a few peas and a few pieces of vegetable marrow, and add to saucepan. Let all this simmer on fire for half an hour, and put away till wanted, when heat up, and serve; but not in the same dish as the rice.

CHAPTER III.

Up Portsmouth Harbour.

SAILING DIRECTIONS.—Small yachts may lie off Southsea Beach, which is shelving, and sheltered from all winds from N.W. round to E.S.E.

If Portsmouth Harbour be preferred, they can lie on the E. side, off the gunwharf, or off Stone Steps on Gosport Hard, below the *Victory*, about 150 yards off the shore.

The Portsmouth Corinthian, and the Albert Yacht Clubs have boat-houses and landing stages on Southsea beach.

The yachtsman lying in any of these berths will find plenty to amuse him ashore in the intervals of runs out to Spithead and down the Solent. During the yachting season Southsea is always lively. The basin or pool inside the shoal, under the beach, is crowded with small craft; there are continually races or regattas afoot, and the piers, the esplanade, and the beach are in full possession of the tripper and holiday-maker of every class. There are naval reviews or manœuvres at Spithead, and military evolutions on the Common. Portsmouth boasts two theatres, where good companies play during the season; and excellent military bands perform daily on the piers. The town itself, however, has little of historical interest to offer.

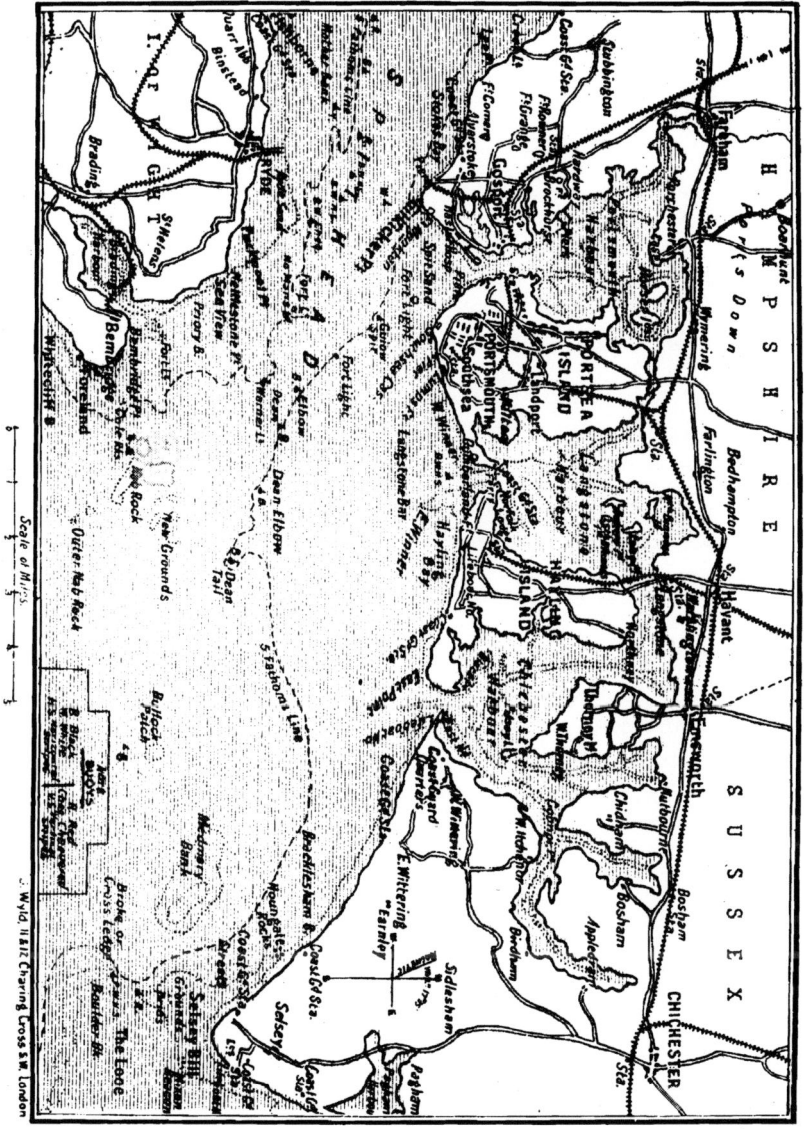

THE SOLENT AND POOLE HARBOUR.

The importance of Portsmouth dates only from Tudor times. Previously Porchester, at the head of the harbour, an important fortress even in Roman times, was the real centre. In Henry VIII.'s reign (see chapter v.) a large French fleet collected off Brading, and was attacked by one from Portsmouth under Lord Lisle, the king himself being encamped with his army on Southsea Common. An indecisive action took place, and one of the largest of the English vessels, the *Rose Mary*, heeled over and sank, much in the same way as the *Royal George* did 250 years later, and her commander, Sir George Carey, was drowned.

The Duke of Buckingham, James I.'s notorious favourite, was murdered at Portsmouth on the eve of his departure to raise the siege of La Rochelle, at No. 12, High Street, part of which still remains.

Charles II. was married to Catherine of Braganza in the hall of the King's House, now part of the Garrison Chapel, a fine building. The register of the marriage is preserved at St. Thomas's, the only old church in Portsmouth, but much pulled about. It contains a monument to the Duke of Buckingham, with his heart in the centre one of three marble urns.

The *Victory*, Nelson's flagship, on board which he died at the battle of Trafalgar, and now the flagship of the Admiral Commander-in-Chief, lies in Portsmouth Harbour, and should be visited. October 21st is the special date, but every Sunday a service is held there which can be attended.

The Dockyard can be visited between ten and twelve. The entrance is close to Portsmouth Harbour station, through an ancient gateway. The Naval College, Admiralty House, and the residences of the naval officials, commonly called Harmony Row, are first passed. Thence through a series of yards between ancient red-brick ranges of buildings, where old anchors, boats, and figure-heads lie rusting and rotting; the mast-house, rope-house, rigging-stores, sail-lofts, to the dry dock, building slips, wood mills, steam basin, and steam factory. All kinds of machinery, from the Nasmyth hammer downwards, may be seen at work in iron and wood. If one of the great white Indian troop-ships is lying at anchor off the jetty, it is well worth a visit. Beyond lie the extension works, with the fitting and repairing basins, and the deep docks, where steam-cranes, hoists, shears, engines, and trains are at work. These works have been excavated from the harbour, chiefly by convict labour from the prison adjoining the dockyard, and from the mud has been formed Whale Island, now the headquarters of the Gunnery School.

A sail up Portsmouth Harbour may be taken to Fareham and Porchester, and gives some idea of the inner sea and land defences of Portsmouth, which, including the outer and sea defences of both ends of the Solent, have cost over two millions of money. The entrance to the harbour is guarded by the Saluting Platform, backed by the old elms of Governor's Green. Opposite are Forts Blockhouse and Monkton. On the left, as you go up the harbour, are the towers and gardens of Haslar Naval Hospital, then the Victualling Yard and the Magazines. Behind, a line of land forts guard Gosport, and join hands above Fareham with the Portsdown forts on the chalk range at the head of the estuary.

To Fareham.

Sailing Directions.—Follow the line of the river past the condemned hulks on the port side, off the Hardway, into Fareham Creek, which is beaconed, or boomed all the way, and is navigable at H.W. for vessels up to 300 tons. The best berth is off Fareham Quay, opposite the fort, where small-class boats can lie afloat even at L.W.

Fareham River is picturesque, with the well-timbered park of Cams Hall (Mr. Delmé) sloping down to the water's edge, but there is little of interest in the town itself.

But two miles West of Fareham Station, in the beautiful valley of the Meon, stands Titchfield, a small market-town, well worth a visit on account of its Norman and Perpendicular church, with the monuments of the Southampton family, and the neighbouring remains of Titchfield House, or Funtley Abbey, Lord Southampton's "right statelie house." It was built by Henry VIII.'s Chancellor Wriothesley on the site of an abbey founded in Henry III.'s reign. A fine gate-house, with turrets and sundry gabled pinnacled remains are all that is left of the "right statelie house embatayled and having a goodlie gate and a conducte (conduit) castelid in the middle of the court of yt. in the very place where the late monastery stood." Here Edward VI. was entertained, and here Charles I. rested after his escape from Hampton Court. Pepys visited Titchfield, and it was Rachel, Lady Russell's birthplace, and the home of her girlhood.

Returning from Fareham down the river, the North Channel leads to Porchester.

Sailing Directions.—Opposite the Hardway, where are two men-of-war, turn into the Porchester Lake, or North Channel, leaving beacon at point to port. You can land at the Castle Hard at any time of tide. At Paul's Grove, where the chalk is loaded, there is a jetty, and one fathom at L.W.

The North Channel leads past Tipnor Magazine and Horsey Island to Porchester Castle, whose massive encincture and square Tudor keep lie at the head of the harbour under the chalk hills, forming a strange link between fortifications of the past and present.

Porchester Castle is undoubtedly of Roman origin, as the red tiles found in the walls testify. In those days, doubtless, the harbour was navigable for triremes and galleys of some size even up to the Water-gate. It is excellently placed on a peninsula, and its walls enclose a square of eight acres, are surmounted with eighteen towers at intervals, defended by a ditch, and entered by the Water-gate and Landport Gate. In the outer bailey is the parish church, an interesting Norman structure, with noticeable font. Originally cruciform, the South transept has been allowed to fall into decay. A many-arched barbican gate leads into the inner bailey, where stands the massive keep. Notice the Roman inscriptions built into the wall right of the entrance. From the summit of the keep there is a bird's-eye view of Portsmouth and Langston Harbour away to Chichester. The church was that of a priory of Black or Austin canons, founded by Henry I., but removed almost immediately to Southwick just over the down.

Porchester is mentioned in the Anglo-Saxon Chronicle as being in the possession of one Portha, 501, who made himself lord of the district. King John made it a frequent starting point for his numerous voyages. It was held by Simon de Montfort's son for his father, as constable of the castle; was often visited by Edward II., and Margaret of Anjou landed here to be married to Henry VII. at Southwick Priory. During the Napoleonic wars it was used as a prison.

A pleasant walk over the down between the grassy casemates of Fort Nelson, past the obelisk 120 feet high raised to the memory of that hero by the survivors of Trafalgar, leads to Southwick Park (T. Thistlewaite, Esq.), a fine place on the borders of the Forest of Bere. In the park are the remains of the Priory. In the former mansion, burnt down, Charles I. was visiting when he heard of Buckingham's murder. North an unrailroaded district of down, forest, deep lane and combe, hop-ground, and ancient homestead, stretching away to Winchester, Alresford, White's Selborne, and Petersfield.

A return route may be taken by Boarhunt, an interesting little Early English church with Saxon work in chancel.

CHAPTER IV.

To Langston Harbour, Hayling Island, and up Chichester Harbour.

SAILING DIRECTIONS.—The bar nearly dries at L.W. About 12 feet over it at H.W. ordinary tides. East and West Winner gravel banks dry one mile from entrance; they frequently shift and have heavy breakers on them in bad weather. There is 8 feet over both banks at H.W. springs.

From Southsea keep under beach close to castle, then allow a ¼ mile from shore. Steer for Fairway Buoy, conical, with black and white horizontal stripes moored in about 11 feet at L.W. springs just inside bar and about 1½ cables N.E. from the highest part of West Winner Bank. Haslar Hospital kept just open South of Southsea Castle about N.W. leads South of both Winner Banks in 9 feet at L.W.

The tide makes into the harbour at 5 o'clock full, and changes and out at 12 o'clock. It runs very hard between entrance points. Best time to run up is one hour before H.W. After passing shore to Fairway Buoy, steer in between entrance points. Water will deepen to 6 and 4 feet just inside. In turning up to entrance back very short, as both Winner banks are steep to. Anchor opposite coastguard. Further up it is impossible to land except at H.W. At the ferry on the Hayling side there is a sandy beach. Small craft can lie in Sineh Lake, just above, and float at any tide if not more than ten feet draught.

The great attraction of Hayling Island are the golf-links and the beautiful sands. The island itself, about four miles long, is joined to the mainland by a swing bridge traversed by a branch of the L.B.S.C.R. from Havant. It is flat but well wooded. The Salterns at North Hayling, to the N.W. of the island, are mentioned in Domesday Book as belonging to the abbey of Jumièges, which had a priory here. The only remains of the latter are in the grounds of the manor house (Misses Padwick), a dove-cote and a long manorial barn with roof built of shipwreck oak. A round moated encampment to the S.E. on the coast is called Tonnorbury, probably from the Saxon god Thor. Both the churches of North and South Hayling are Early English, and very interesting. That of South Hayling is of flint. At South Hayling the double piscina in chancel, and another in South aisle, and the great yew in the churchyard should be noticed. Oyster culture is the great industry of the island. During severe winter the ponds are thawed by a steam engine, and by fires round the edges. A ferry leads across Langston Harbour mouth to Fort Cumberland, and thence into Southsea.

Up Chichester Harbour.

Sailing Directions.—Coming out of Langston Harbour, steer for Langston Buoy to clear the East Winner Bank. Then follow the line of the bay, giving a fair berth of $\frac{1}{4}$ mile. Anchoring off Hayling Beach, sheltered from N.W., you can land anywhere, except in West wind, on good sandy beach.

Follow the beach with berth of 200 yards, till Chichester Harbour opens. It is difficult of access, as banks off it (East and West Pole) are constantly shifting. The bar has only 2 feet on it at L.W. springs, and a shoal flat extends off 2 miles.

East Pole gravel banks, dry $1\frac{1}{2}$ miles outside East point of entrance, and West Pole runs out $\frac{1}{4}$ mile from West entrance point. When there is any swell on outside, the sea breaks heavily over the banks and across the entrance, especially with South winds on the ebb.

The tides turn about same time as Langston, and run hard between the points, and over the bar when the banks are uncovered. The entrance lies 5 miles N.E. from Nab Lightship. To preserve a proper offing till tide time, keep Haslar Hospital just open off Southsea Castle, and you will have three fathoms at L.W. The ground is everywhere clean.

To enter, keep the Watchhouse on East entrance point N.E. by E. $\frac{1}{4}$ E. until water deepens, when steer in between entrance points.

The Emsworth Channel to port-hand is beaconed all the way, but is best taken at half flood when the channel shows.

Anchor off point of Thorney Island, where there is a hard. Further up the channel there is no water at L.W., and you ground. At the Thorney Point mentioned there is a hard on both hands.

The similarity of the low land of peninsulas and islands, of creeks and estuaries, lying between the Sussex Downs and the Channel with the fen country, is further exemplified by the presence of a Thorney Island in both. To the Thorney Island of the South, however, belongs the glory of having produced the first English poet. Caedmon

TO THE SOLENT AND POOLE HARBOUR.

was born here, and seems to have attracted the notice of St. Wilfred, the apostle of the South Saxons, who evangelized all the country about Bosham, building the first Christian Church in these parts at Selsey. He was Bishop of Ripon, in Yorkshire, and president of the celebrated council which met at Whitby to decide upon the date of keeping Easter. Probably it was he who transplanted Caedmon to the North, where we find him serving as ferry-man at St. Hilda's Abbey, a craft he was more likely to have learnt on the inland waters of Thorney than on the rough Northumbrian coast. At St. Hilda's Abbey the " Milton of our forefathers," as he has been called, composed in his sleep his celebrated hymn or paraphrase of the creation, now in the Bodleian Library, at Oxford.

Thorney Island is quite flat, but well wooded. A causeway now joins it to the mainland near Emsworth. The manor house is the residence of the Padwick family, the principal landowners. The church has been recently restored; it is remarkable for its great length, and contains some good Norman and Early English work, and two leper windows. The priest's door, blocked up for centuries, is Norman, and the view through it under the old elms to the blue water beyond is a very pretty peep. An Early English arch leads to the strong tower, lighted by lancet windows, and divided from the nave by an old twelfth-century screen, and containing a rude Norman font. In the old smuggling days Thorney Church tower was used as a *cache*, whence the inhabitants drew their ill-gotten casks into Emsworth in carts with india-rubber tyres, having previously towed them into the harbour under water by means of a rope through a hollow tiller. Two curious pillars in the walls where the South aisle stood, the South door with its rich dog-tooth carving, the ancient twelfth-century chancel screen, and the curious slabs of tombs (one carved with a crozier), some used as foundations, and the fine roof, are the principal points of interest in this fine old church.

An attempt was made to run a dam across the entrance of the Thorney or Prinstead Channel, to unite the island to the eastern mainland, and to reclaim the channel. But one stormy night the sea broke in over the embankment, and the men on watch had to run for their lives, and a row of skeleton posts now marks the site of the works. Pilsey Island, a mere mound of shingle, was once the habitation of a modern hermit, who, however, probably was but a smuggler in disguise.

There is nothing to see of interest in Emsworth, a fifth-rate little port, in which every third house seems to be a public-house. It lies on the numerous *rythes* or channels of the tide, and has some considerable industry in the oyster-beds, partly stocked by native fish and partly by imported.

About a mile and a half along the Havant road at the head of this branch of Chichester Haven lies Warblington, with a very ancient church, with Early English and Decorated work, said to have been built by two maiden ladies, the last of the line of the Warblingtons, who lived in the castle close by, of which only a tower remains. Originally a quadrangle surrounded by a moat, and with a square keep, it was demolished during the Civil Wars. Here, during the reign of Henry VII., was immured the Countess of Salisbury, mother of Reginald Pole.

To Bosham.

Sailing Directions.—Come down the Emsworth Channel, the latter part or the last quarter of ebb, or wait till half tide or H.W., almost to the harbour mouth. The Bosham Channel past Pilsey Island and Cobnor Point is beaconed all the way; and if you go up with the tide, the channel is easily seen. But look out for Cobnor Point. In Bosham Deep, close to land, small craft can lie afloat even at L.W.

Between Cobnor and Itchnor Points, names betokening a Danish origin with the ending " or," the yachtsman will pass over the celebrated Bell Hole, the scene of the following legend of the lost bell of Bosham. The monks of the Bosham Monastery had, it seemed, waxed lax in their duties, and as a punishment their patron saint, St. Nicholas, let the Norsemen loose upon them. The Vikings sailed up to Bosham Deep, and, plundering the village and the monastery, carried off with them, as a trophy, the tenor bell from Bosham steeple. No sooner, however, had their dragon-prowed galleys sailed away down the estuary, than the penitent monks fell on their knees in the church, and caused a thanksgiving peal to be rung from the Saxon tower with the seven remaining bells. But, lo! and behold, from down across the harbour rang the tenor bell in answer to its brethren, and just as they sailed past Itchnor Point the horrified Vikings saw the hold of their galley open, and the bell descend into the water, the ship closing up behind it again. St. Nicholas had evidently no mind that the holy bell fell permanently into heathen hands. To him the monks prayed that he would restore it to them again. In a dream to one of their number, he consented, if they could find a team of milk-white oxen with which to draw it up from the watery depths. An attempt was made, but it failed, as one of the oxen had a black hair in his tail, and to this day there are only seven bells in Bosham steeple. But, if you are sailing over the Bell Hole when the Bosham bells are ringing, you may still hear the lost bell answering from the depths below, at least so the legend says. Further, the Bosham people are much offended if you venture to address them by their local opprobrious nickname of "Ding-dongs." The truth of the matter is, that at the Bell Hole, a worn circular hole at the confluence of the Chichester and Bosham Channels, there is a remarkable echo with Itchnor Point, and it is a well-known fact in acoustics that if you strike a third and a fifth, the echo of the octave follows.

Bosham, or Bosenham, the "Town of the Wood," lies picturesquely on Bosham Deep, name suggestive again of the fen country. Red-tiled houses, spars and masts, an ancient windmill, and huge old yew-trees group around the conical Sussex spire of the venerable church, the whole backed by the bold green outline of the downs. Nearly two thousand years ago Bosham was a more stirring place than it is now. Three miles off across the meadows lay Regnum (Chichester), the Aldershot of Vespasian, and full of Roman remains even at this day. On the site of the present church of Bosham he built a basilica or courthouse, and the bases of the present chancel arches are undoubtedly Roman. Quantities of Roman tiles, bricks, and pottery have been found under the nave, and fragments are to be traced in the walls. When St. Wilfrid began to christianize Sussex in 681, the monastery of Bosham, mentioned by Bede, was one of the centres of missionary effort. The brethren were of the order of S. Benedict, and the rule was very strict. In the map of the

Anglo-Saxon chronicle, Bosham is one of the only five places marked in Sussex. A little later it was a favourite residence of Canute, one of whose children was buried in the church, which he probably built. The monastery and manor, however, passed from the Archbishopric of Canterbury to Earl Godwin, Canute's son-in-law, by a shameless fraud. The rapacious Earl, whose possessions were already very large, went with an armed band to pay his court to the Archbishop, and to ask for the kiss of peace. "Da mihi Boseam," begged the kneeling Earl. The Archbishop, thinking he said "Basium," replied "Da tibi." Whereon the crafty Earl, with profuse thanks, hurried off to take possession of the manor of Bosham. He built a hall there, probably where the present old Manor House stands, north of the church, for the moat remains, and part of the material of the house is of great antiquity. Harold, his unlucky son, succeeded to the whole tract of country round Bosham. He figures in the Bayeux tapestry, as embarking, hawk on wrist, from Bosham for Normandy. In the background is the identical Saxon chancel arch of the present church. In the Domesday Book we find the little hermitage planted by the Scottish monk Dieül, Wilfrid's co-labourer, had grown into one of the most affluent foundations in the country; and in the fourteenth century we find the town itself as of greater importance than Arundel; for the Duke of Norfolk's feudary book mentions that six fairs were annually held there, but at Arundel only three. Becket's secretary and biographer, Herbert de Bosham, was born at Bosham. He retired to Italy after his master's death, becoming eventually Archbishop of Benevento. A tomb in the southern aisle is pointed out as Herbert's tomb. He was a distinguished scholar, and his most popular work, *Vita Sancti Thomae*, is still preserved at Cambridge.

About the reign of Edward IV. Bosham Manor passed to the Duke of Norfolk; thence in 1475 to the Barons of Berkeley, one of the oldest families in the country, who still own it. In 1665 the plague attacked Chichester, which was "boycotted" by the country side, and whose inhabitants would have starved but for the assistance of the Bosham men, who supplied them each day with provisions, which they placed on a spot outside the town, and retreated, the citizens of Chichester coming out with the money for them, which they placed in a stone water-trough to avoid infection.

South of the church are some remains of the ancient college of Bosham, founded *temp.* Henry I., notably a thick wall, with a pointed doorway. Within the enclosure was dug up a gigantic stone head of Woden, or S. Christopher, or Trajan, now in the Bishop's Palace at Chichester.

The church itself consists of a Saxon tower, externally doorless, very thick and strong and dim, with a notable nave window, Saxon nave, and the Saxon chancel arch aforementioned. The chancel, which ends in an apse, is Early English lengthened in the 12th century out of the original chancel, with an Early English five-light east window. In the South aisle is a groined Early English crypt, adjoining Herbert's tomb, used as a storehouse in the days of free trade, when much good French brandy found its surreptitious way over Chichester Bar to Bosham. When the church was restored in 1865, the stone coffin of a child was found at the spot under the chancel arch, where tradition laid the burial place of Canute's daughter.

To Chichester.

Sailing Directions.—For Chichester go East at Cobnor Point. The channel is very narrow and shallow. You can lie at Copperas Point in 4 feet of water at S.W., and row to Dull Quay, where there is a jetty and a hard.

From Dull Quay strike across the meadows to the road for Chichester, where there is much to be seen. Four straight streets converge on to the Market Cross (the gift of a bishop of the fifteenth century), and plainly demonstrate the Roman origin of the town, which was of great importance in Roman Britain, as Regnum. The Conqueror gave it and three adjoining manors to Roger de Montgomery, who built the castle, of which no traces remain. The cathedral dates from the same period, when the bishopric was removed from Selsey. It has been much restored and altered during the present century. In 1861 the North spire, supported on a tower and four piers, suddenly collapsed entirely during a great gale, but without injuring the rest of the building. It was rebuilt by Sir G. G. Scott. The detached campanile, or bell tower, the only example in England in connection with a cathedral, is Perpendicular 15th century. The cathedral itself is open daily without payment. A detailed account of it would be foreign to this work, but the following points of interest should not be omitted :—

The *West Porch*, very beautiful Early English. The *four aisles* of the nave, quite unique in an English cathedral, though common abroad, and producing beautiful effects. The *North nave*, with later clerestory. The *plain arches* and rude capitals of the *first two stories* of the *South-West tower*, probably of an earlier date than the rest of the building. The *Arundel Chantry*, with much-mutilated effigies, repaired in 1843. The *Chapel of S. John the Baptist* at the end of the North aisle, with fine decorated tomb of an unknown lady. In the nave and North aisle 10 *Flaxman Monuments*. The long, narrow *Norman Choir;* the 14th century *window in the South transept*. The *tomb in the same of a holy bishop, S. Richard of Chichester,* 1245, a famous place of mediæval pilgrimage, where miracles were said to be worked. In the same transept *a 16th century picture* representing the Saxon King Ceadwalla bestowing Selsey on S. Wilfrid. The *ancient consistory court* over the South porch, late Perpendicular, with the original president's chair, and communicating by a sliding panel with an archive chamber called "The Lollard's Prison." The *sacristy, Early English*. In the *South aisle, two* uncommon sculptured stone *slabs,* early Norman, said to have been removed from Selsey. In the *Retro-choir the four detached Purbeck shafts,* unique; the *bosses* on the *vaulting ribs,* especially one of six human faces, near the South aisle. The beautiful *Lady Chapel*. The treasures of the *Cathedral library,* both of books and plate. The *decorations of the North transept,* by Bernardi, an Italian artist of the 16th century, who similarly adorned all the vaultings, but whose work was destroyed by Waller's soldiers after the town was taken by the Parliamentarians in 1643, when nearly every scrap of paint was scraped off, and every effigy and image mutilated. The *cloisters,* irregular in shape and position, lead to the *Bishop's Palace,* with a late Early English chapel, and more decorations by Bernardi.

The old Refectory of the Vicars of the Cathedral, now used as a girls' school, contains the high table on the dais, the rostrum for the reader, and the lavatorium. Below is the old Guildhall granted by Edward III. to the Vicars, and which stretched across the street.

St. Mary's Hospital, 12th century, supports eight poor people. The long hall with wide roof resting on massive wooden timbers, contained rooms of two cubicles each for the inmates; a decorated open oak screen divides it from the chapel.

The church of S. Olave is on the site of a Roman building, as urns and bricks were found in its walls during restoration, and is probably the earliest Christian Church in Chichester.

The Guildhall was the chapel of the Grey Friars. It is Early English, with a fine East window and sedilia. In the garden is a mound, probably the remains of the Norman keep.

Under S. Andrew's Church is a Roman pavement. In the Vicar's College in South Street, now a schoolroom, is an ancient lavatory and rostrum. The city walls, chiefly of Roman flints, and with towers at intervals, form pleasant walks to the North and East.

From Chichester, an interesting excursion, amid lovely scenery, may be made among the beautifully wooded hill country to Goodwood House and race-course—about three miles. The house, in its lovely park, is open to visitors, except during the race week, and contains fine pictures. A round may be made through the park up to the race-course, through the famous beech-woods, returning on the West side to another gate. The views of Hampshire and Sussex—the sea and the Isle of Wight—are very beautiful, and the trees are magnificent, especially the Lebanon cedars, planted to the number of 1,000 in 1761. The largest, near the dog-kennels, measures 25 feet in circumference. There are two large cork-trees

D

near the principal entrance lodge, and a chestnut grove in the High Wood. Not far from the house is a temple, where is kept the famous Neptune and Minerva slab, found at Chichester in 1731, and carved with the inscription which seems to link Regnum with the Claudia and Pudens mentioned by St. Paul and Martial. It formed part of a Roman temple dedicated to those deities.

The celebrated Goodwood race week is the last week in July, and is patronised by royalty, who are generally entertained by the Duke of Richmond at the House.

East of Goodwood, and nearer Chichester, lies West Hampnett, with Early English church and curious Pietà monument. West Hampnett Place, now the union workhouse, is an Elizabethan house, with the great staircase ceiling, painted by Kneller, built by an ancestor of the Delawarr family.

Two miles further on is Boxgrove, with interesting remains of the Priory founded in Henry I.'s reign. The Parish Church consists of the chancel, aisles and transepts, and central tower of the Priory Church, and is all Norman or Early English. The choir is especially graceful and beautiful, the vaulting being painted in the same style as Chichester Cathedral. It was beautified by Lord Delawarr, whose tomb should be noticed. Outside are the ruins of the nave, the chapter-house and cloisters; also the pigeon-house, prior's lodgings, and other domestic offices.

In Halnaker Park, 1½ miles further on, are the ruins of a Henry VIII. mansion, built by Lord Delawarr, and a fine chestnut avenue.

CHAPTER V.

To Bembridge and Brading Harbour.

SAILING DIRECTIONS.—Course from Chichester Bar to Bembridge Fort. W. by S. ½ S., distance seven miles. Leave Fort on port hand, make Fairway Buoy at the entrance to Harbour. Flagstaff on Spithead Hotel, Bembridge, and Bembridge Church spire in line, will lead over bar and into the old channel, which is well buoyed up to the harbour, with black and chequered buoy. As long as no rocks are seen round the base of Bembridge Fort there will not be less than nine feet of water anywhere with the above leading mark on.

Try to get a mooring in the harbour, as the holding ground is very bad, and the gush heavy with S.W. or W. winds.

The Bar is nearly awash with L.W. springs. The bottom in this channel is rocky. The New Channel is only forty feet wide, and is well boomed. Tide runs like a mill-race; and though there are four feet in it at L.W., a stranger would do better to wait till there was water in Old Channel. The bank fronting entrance is steep to. Land at pier, beach H.W., or ferry on opposite side for the links.

Bembridge Harbour is all that remains of the wide, shallow estuary of the eastern Yar known as Brading Harbour. At one time (as was proved by the discovery, during the reclamation works of the seventeenth century, of a stone-cased well in the middle of the haven) a broad expanse of meadow land, it was overflowed by the sea during historical times. The legend runs that the greedy discoverers annexed, by means of magic, vast treasures hidden in the well, and that, as a consequence or a punishment, the sea poured in and submerged the district. From the reign of Edward I. downwards, efforts have been made to reclaim Brading Haven, and the Yar now flows narrow and sluggish through a wide expanse of meadow, marsh and mud, to the sluice gates at the head of Bembridge Harbour, crossed both by road and by a branch of the Ryde and Ventnor Railway.

Bembridge is the headquarters of the Bembridge Sailing Club, whose single-handed half-raters are well known in the Solent. The little Club House stands on the left shore of the harbour near the pier, and the peculiarly rigged Club boats lie moored in the basin below.

The "Spithead Hotel," a fine building adjoining the pier, is the headquarters of the Bembridge Golf Club. Their links, considered one of the most sporting in the British Isles, lie on what was known as St. Helen's, Dover, or Duvver, the local name for Strand, under the wooded heights of St. Helen's, on the right of the harbour mouth. The principal matches at Christmas and at Easter attract golfers from all parts of the kingdom, and St. Andrew's Day is celebrated by a club dinner at the "Spithead Hotel."

The golf and sailing clubs combine to make Bembridge an attractive but somewhat select watering-place during the summering months. There is not a great choice of villas or lodging-houses, and these are chiefly of an old-fashioned type. Several times a day steamers ply in summer between Bembridge and the new pier, Southsea.

The church is modern. Bembridge is an interesting centre for walks or drives. A walk up the village, along a shady road, between villa gardens, to the sandy chine on the shore, may be continued along the cliffs to the Foreland, the easternmost point of the Island. Thence through a quiet rural country overlooking Whitecliffe Bay, which is extremely interesting to the geologist as abounding in Eocene fossils and exhibiting extraordinarily subverted strata. It is bounded on the S.W. by the chalk Culver Cliff, above which rises the rounded summit of Bembridge Down capped with its square fort, one of the chain which guard the East end of the Island and the entrance to the Solent. From the Down the path dips down into a lane leading to Yaverland Manor House, and the tiny Early English church it overshadows. This beautiful specimen of Jacobean domestic architecture, one of the best in an island especially rich in such remains, stands charmingly "under the ridge of a noble down," its ivy-covered gables backed by ancient elms, and commands a fine prospect of sea and down. Now merely a farmhouse, it was once the seat of one of the most ancient and powerful of the Island families, and was the *Stam-schloss* (root-castle), in fact, of the now ducal house of Bedford. The church (Edward I.) was built by Sir William Russell, who found the frequent floods of the Yar interfered with his devotions at Brading, but who eventually bridged the stream, whence the name Bembridge or Withinbridge. The little edifice has been carefully restored, and contains a fine Norman door and chancel arch. Legh Richmond was sometime curate here. From Yaverland the return route to Bembridge may be taken along the slopes of the Yar valley, past Centurion's or S. Urian's Coppice.

From Bembridge the train (changing at St. Helen's Junction) may be taken to Brading, Sandown, Shanklin, and Ventnor. The first-named, "the Kynge's towne of Bradinge," standing on the hill above the strath, is a very ancient corporate town, dating from Edward VI., and still governed by a bailiff, recorder, etc. The whipping-post, stocks, and bull-ring, a relic of bull-baiting, are still shown. The fine church, late Norman and Early English, contains curious altar-tombs, chiefly of the Oglander family. In the churchyard is the grave of Legh Richmond's "Young Cottager."

Two miles beyond Brading, just off the Sandown Road, under the southern slope of Brading Down, are the remains of a Roman villa, probable date A.D. 250, excavated in 1880, and lying but a few inches below the soil. Many of the principal suites of rooms, corridors, and picture galleries have been uncovered. The hypocaust, or heating chamber, bath and well, can be traced. The mosaic pavement is the especial glory of this English Pompeii. The medallions represent mythological subjects; one of them, a man with a cock's head and claws, is evidently a caricature, and may have been intended for a skit on the reigning Emperor Galienus.

West of Brading, and North of the Downs, lies Nunwell (Lady Oglander). The Oglander family came over at the Conquest from Oglandes in Normandy. The widow of the last baronet resides at Nunwell. The house, modern, stands in a well-timbered park. The trees are finer than are usually found in this part of the Island, much denuded of timber during the Napoleonic wars for ship-building in Portsmouth Dockyard. The pedestrian from Brading along the lane can walk through the park up on to the Down, and down it back into

Brading, securing a fine view of all the East portion of the Island.

The Bembridge end of "the invincible isle," as Drayton has it, has more than once been the scene of French invasions. As early as 1310 Sir John de Lisle, of Wootton, the then Captain, or Warden, of the Island, divided it into military districts, to be guarded by the principal landowners and their men. This was indeed not unnecessary. In 1340 the French landed at St. Helen's Point, and pressed forward into the interior, to find the bridge over the Yar broken down to impede them, and to be repulsed and driven back to their ships by Sir Theobald Russell, Lord of Yaverland, who fell in the struggle. In July, 1545, several unsuccessful attempts on other parts of the Island having intervened, a large French fleet, under D'Annebault, anchored in a line almost from Brading Harbour to Ryde. Fourteen English vessels stood out from Portsmouth under Lord Lisle, and one of the most important naval engagements that had taken place for centuries ensued. The French treasure ship, disabled, lay abandoned ashore at the mouth of Brading Harbour. Next day the French landed close to Bembridge, destroyed the fort at Seaview, on the point still called Old Fort, and penetrated as far as the Culver Cliffs, harassed by the English, but covered by the fire from the fleet. D'Annebault hesitated whether to attack Portsmouth, or to seize and fortify the Island with the 7,000 pioneers he had brought with him for that purpose. Finally he sheered off out of the Solent altogether into Sandown Bay, where the party sent ashore for water under the *Chevalier d'Eulx* were all killed in an ambuscade in the Chine.

CHAPTER VI.

To Seaview, Ryde, Wootton Creek and Cowes.

SAILING DIRECTIONS. — Coming out at H.W., clear Bembridge Fort on port hand, and steer for the end of Seaview Pier. Off this you can anchor and land at pier in all tides, and at flood on the rocky beach. There are various holes round the pierhead, affording good anchorage.

When coming out of Seaview at ebb run off to the Norman Fort, which is chequered. Leave it close on starboard, and steer for Sand Head Buoy, chequered, then for the end of Ryde Pier in line with Quarr Abbey House on the hill above Wootton Creek. This will clear Ryde Sand.

Ryde is but an open roadstead. Small craft can pick up any of the many moorings about, and anchor E. or W. off pierhead, but not nearer in, according to wind. On the East side anchor close to pier, as the mud bank runs down. If necessary, run for Portsmouth Harbour or Wootton Creek.

From Ryde to Wootton Creek follow the coast inside the Quarantine Hulks to the triangular boom at the mouth of the creek, and go up at H.W., or till Wootton Rocks West of this boom are covered, where there will be five feet of water in the channel. Leave triangular boom to starboard. The best water is within twenty feet of this. The second boom is parallel to the one on starboard, the third must be left to port. Channel then winds to West, and the next boom is left on the starboard. The following boom, opposite the coastguard station, marks the corner of mud. Now allow channel to be twenty yards broad, and keep near vessels moored here on their buoys on North side. The best water is ten feet outside them. Opposite a boat-house to port a corner runs out, so leave wide berth to starboard. Beyond is a picturesque and sheltered pool, where small craft can lie afloat at all states of the tide, and larger vessels on soft mud. The tide rises twelve feet. There is a hard, to starboard, and a slip by coastguard at Fishbourne to port, nearer entrance. At H.W. small-class boats can get up to Wootton Mill, lying in mud at L.W. But a row is recommended up this pretty estuary.

The southern shore of the Solent, from St. Helen's Point to Cowes, is but one succession of charming grounds appertaining to the marine mansions and villas that dot the wooded heights—grounds more or less ample in dimensions, but all thickly wooded and sloping to the sea, the undergrowth, ferns, and gigantic primroses growing down to high-water mark in a way peculiar to this mild climate and sheltered arm of the sea. St. Helen's Priory, on the point of that name, is a picturesque mansion on the site of an ancient foundation of Cluniac monks. The old church of St. Helen's, on the Point, was sapped by the sea, and only its tower remains, used as a sea-mark. The present one stands inland, remote alike from sea and village, which latter is grouped round a wide green, the only village green in the Island, on the slope of Brading Harbour.

At Nettlestone Point stands Seaview, a watering-place,

with villas and houses rising in steep tiers from the rocky shore, where at low tide are excellent sands. In the summer steamers ply between Southsea and the Suspension Pier at Seaview. There is a walk for foot passengers all along the shore from Seaview to Ryde, under Puckpool Battery, one of the outer defences which guard Portsmouth Harbour.

Ryde is very full in August, and a crowd of yachts of every size lie round the pierhead, especially during the second week, when the Victoria Yacht Club Regatta takes place. Besides this annual fixture there are continual races for small classes and half-raters taking place, and hardly a day passes but some white-winged racing fleet passes Ryde Pier up or down the Solent. From Ryde Pier rail or coach excursions can be made to all parts of the Island. Hotels: The "Royal Pier," and many others.

Quarr Abbey House (Lady Cochrane), where H.R.H. Prince and Princess Henry of Battenberg spent their honeymoon in 1885, stands on the high ground between Ryde and Wootton Creek. A footpath from Ryde leads past Binstead Church, and the ruins of Quarr Abbey, through Quarr Park, to a cluster of fishing cottages round a neat grass-plot, known as Fishhouse or Fishbourne, and which boasts a post-box and general shop. A little up Wootton Creek is a yacht-building yard and stores (W. and H. Hayles), where boats of every size can be laid up and repaired.

Quarr Abbey.—But few remains, though ivy-grown and picturesque, mark the site of the great Cistercian foundation of the Island. Built in 1132 by Count Baldwin de Redvers, the then Warden, son-in-law of the Conqueror, it contained, among others, the tombs of himself, of Adeliza, his wife, and of Lady Cicely, a daughter of Edward IV., who married, *en secondes noces*, plain John Keime, of Standen Manor, under St. George's Down. The Abbot of Quarr was an important person; he held manors all over the Island. In 1340 the Abbey was strongly fortified. At the dissolution it was bought by a Southampton merchant, and practically razed to the ground. Its precincts, covering some forty acres, can still be traced by the ivy-mantled walls. Near the shore the sea-gate still exists, and the infirmary chapel and other parts have been built into a Jacobean farmhouse. In 1891 Quarr was partially excavated by Mr. Percy Stone, F.S.A. Digging but a few feet below the soil, he was able to determine the infirmary, with its hall of three alleys and its hearths; the cloisters, with their pillars of Purbeck marble (largely used throughout the building); the Frater, the lavatorium, and the unique chapter-house, with its slender Purbeck shafts and delicate vaulting ribs. The church itself, a vast and magnificent building, stood where the road now runs past the farmhouse, West of the brook. Specimens of tiles, and of the *grisaille* glass used in the severe Cistercian architecture, were found; also two skeletons, one that of a female, in the North wall, near the high altar, which Mr. Stone considers to be those of the founder and his wife.

Wootton village lies round the bridge which crosses the creek at the mill about a mile from the sea. All supplies but meat can be obtained there. Wootton Church, a small, ancient edifice, with good Norman door, stands on high ground three-quarters of a mile west of the village. The manor-farm adjoining is on the site of the manor-house of the De Lisles, a powerful island family, one of whom, Sir William Lisle, brother of the regicide, is buried in the church. He was a staunch Cavalier and companion in exile of Charles II. His widow, Dame Alice Lisle, was executed at the age of eighty for sheltering adherents of Monmouth.

Sailing Directions. — Wootton to Cowes. Follow Osborne Bay to Old Castle Point Buoy. Then steer for the Squadron Club House on opposite point. Make the red and white chequered buoy, leave on port hand, and turn into harbour ; steer for pontoon, and lie opposite it out of the way of steamers, or off East Cowes Coastguard, in a pool frequented by coasters.

King's Quay is a small muddy inlet in Osborne Bay, bounding to East the royal demesne, embedded in oak coppices,—a lonely spot, the haunt of wild-fowl, and crossed by a picturesque lane from Wootton to Osborne, at Deadman's Hollow. The legend runs that **King John** sheltered here three months from his barons. In Elizabeth's time King's Quay was the resort of pirates. The inlet is just possible for a row-boat at H.W.

The foreshore of Osborne and Norris Castle are protected by a massive sea wall, as all this coast, composed largely of blue slipper clay, is much encroached upon by the sea. The coastguards have orders to prevent people landing in the demesne.

Osborne being the Queen's private property and not a State residence, Her Majesty jealously guards its privacy. For half a century it has been emphatically the *home* of the Royal Family, and all sorts of associations, sad and sweet, cluster about the trim Italian terraces, the bosky gardens, and the woodland drives of Her Majesty's seaside residence. Decidedly it is from the sea that the best view of Osborne is obtained. The house, with its towers and loggia, its green lawns and glades sweeping to the sea, the dark plantations of rare evergreens, the woods of the Swiss gardens, the roof of the Swiss châlet, and the Queen's kiosque from the Windsor Agricultural Show, can all be made out as one sails by. On the shore stands the bathing-house, and hard by is the little schooner yacht moored, now used chiefly for taking royal grandchildren for a sail. At the landing-place the German Emperor disembarked from his galley, when his fleet, which escorted the Hohenzollern yacht from Germany, anchored in Osborne Bay, and saluted the British standard flying from the towers of Osborne House.

Residents in the neighbourhood can, however, by special card, to be obtained of the steward, gain admittance to Osborne demesne, but not to the private grounds.

Next to Osborne, and even in a more beautiful situation on the wooded slopes of Old Castle Point, rise the pseudo-Gothic battlements of Norris Castle (Duke of Bedford), where the late Emperor Frederick resided during his last visit to England, in the Jubilee year. Here George IV. was entertained, and here Her Majesty occasionally lived with the Duchess of Kent previous to her accession.

East Cowes Castle (Viscount Gort) stands in a park, back from the sea, behind Norris Castle.

About two miles from East Cowes, and three from Wootton Creek, is Whippingham Church, with a few scattered cottages and farmhouses and the Queen's almshouses for the aged poor on Her Majesty's estate. Whippingham makes a nice round either from Cowes Harbour or Wootton Creek. The road by the latter is the prettiest, a deep lane, through coppices and Deadman's Hollow. Whippingham Church is modern, was built by the Prince Consort in a peculiar cruciform style. There are beautiful memorial medallions to him and the Queen's deceased children and grandchildren. Since a private chapel has been built at Osborne, Her Majesty rarely attends service at Whippingham. The view from the churchyard, behind the church, over the valley of the Medina, should not be missed. Near Whippingham, on the road to Wootton through Deadman's Hollow, is Barton Court, with the Prince Consort model farm adjoining. It stands on the site of a very ancient oratory, the curious rules of which are still preserved at Winchester. The House has been rebuilt by Her Majesty in exact imitation of the several fine specimens of Jacobean Manor Houses which exist in the Island. It is surrounded by choice trees and shrubs, noticeably a grove of cork-trees.

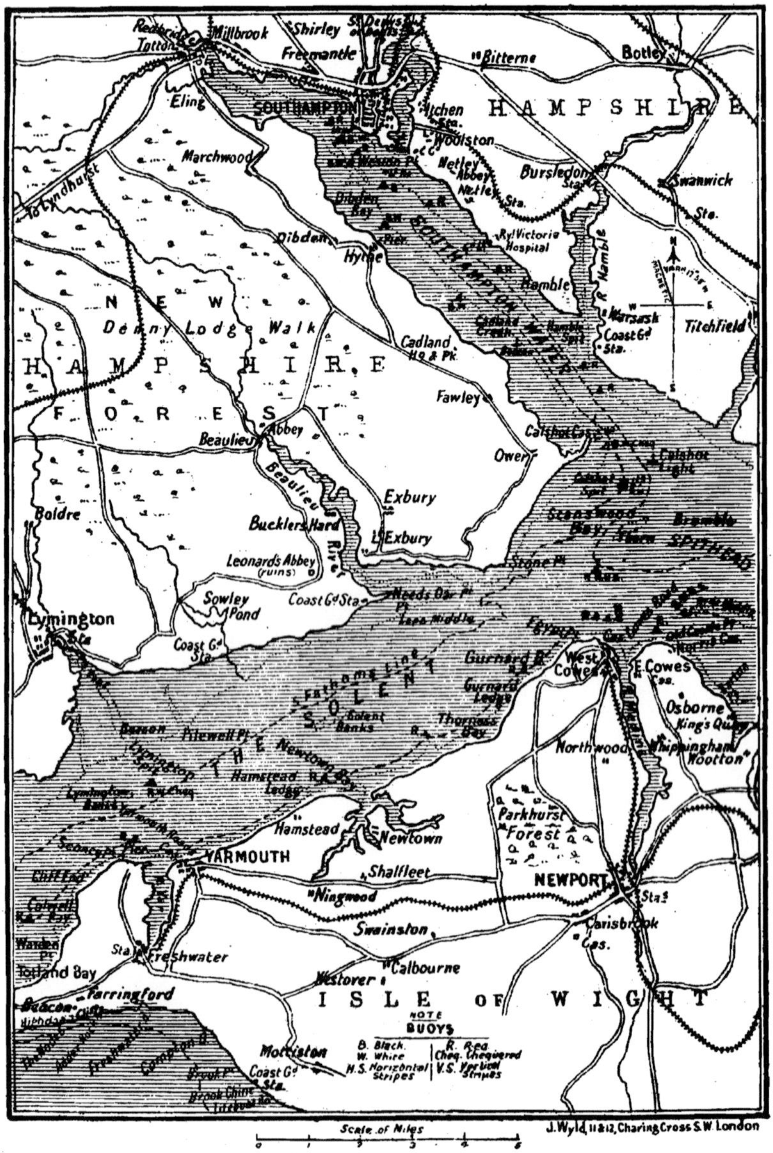

Redbridge
Totton
Millbrook
Shirley
Freemantle
Bitterne
Botley
Eling
SOUTHAMPTON
Itchen Sta.
Woolston
HAMPSHIRE
Marchwood
Netley Abbey
Netley Sta.
Bursledon Sta.
Swanwick Sta.
To Lyndhurst
Dibden Bay
Dibden
Hythe
Pier
SOUTHAMPTON WATER
Ryl Victoria Hospital
Hamble
R. Hamble
Warsash
Coast Gd Sta.
Titchfield
NEW FOREST
Denny Lodge Walk
HAMPSHIRE
Cadland Hd & Pk.
Fawley
Calshot Cas.
Calshot Light
Beaulieu
Abbey
Ower
Beaulieu River
Exbury
Lt. Exbury
Boldre
Bucklers Hard
Stanswood Bay
Bramble
SPITHEAD
Stone Pt.
Leonard's Abbey (ruins)
Sowley Pond
Coast Gd Sta.
Needs Oar Pt.
Lymington
Sta.
Coast Gd. Sta.
Gurnard B.
West Cowes
E. Cowes
Cas.
Gurnard Ledge
Osborne
King's Quay
5 Fathoms Line
THE SOLENT
Solent Banks
Thorness Bay
Pilewell Pt.
Northwood
Whippingham
Wootton
Newtown Bay
Hamstead Ledge
Hamstead
Newtown
Parkhurst Forest
YARMOUTH
Shalfleet
NEWPORT
Stas.
Ningwood
Cliff End
Colwell Bay
Warden Pt.
Swainston
Carisbrook Cas.
Sta.
Freshwater
Totland Bay
Westover
Calbourne
Farringford
Beacon
ISLE OF WIGHT
NOTE
BUOYS
B. Black.
W. White
H.S. Horizontal Stripes
R. Red
Cheq. Chequered
V.S. Vertical Stripes
Mottiston
Coast Gd. Sta.
Brook Pt.
Brook Chine
Compton B.
Scale of Miles
0
1
2
3
4
5
J. Wyld, 11 & 12, Charing Cross S.W. London

CHAPTER VII.

Up the Medina.

SAILING DIRECTIONS.—Take half tide up, which will give you two or three hours in Newport or Carrisbrooke, and the ebb down. Lie off Fairlie on East bank and row up to Newport Quay. At Fairlie there is a hard and a footpath to the high road. Going up with the flood you can lie at Newport Quay on the mud, but the holes are small and crowded.

> " The two great Cows that in loud thunder roar,
> This on the eastern, this on the western shore,
> Where Newport enters stately Wight."
> —*Leland.*

Of these two circular forts, built by Henry VIII., like Hurst Castle, of the materials of Beaulieu Abbey, one remains but in name—Old Castle Point. The other is now converted into the Royal Yacht Squadron Clubhouse. This is the *doyen* of Yacht Clubs. H.R.H. the Prince of Wales is Commodore, and election to it, and to the right to fly the white ensign, and the white burgee, with red cross of the Club, is eagerly sought for, and not easy to accomplish. During the Regatta week, the first week in August, under certain conditions, members may admit visitors into the Club, and ladies into the little garden behind it. There under the tall elms, during the late afternoon, congregate the cream of English society, the *élite* of the yachting world, while the private landing stage below the miniature battery, which announces the beginning and the conclusion of each race, is beset by gigs and launches from the long line of yachts moored right across the estuary of the Medina almost from **Egypt House** to **Old Castle Point**. From a racing point of view, however, there is nothing special in the Squadron Regatta, which barely holds its own with the younger and more enterprising clubs.

The Royal London Yacht Club have a Cowes house on the Parade, much frequented in August.

At high water it is a pleasant sail up the Medina to Newport Quay (where there is six feet of water at high tide), past the shipbuilding yards, where craft of all kinds, including torpedo boats, are turned out. Of late yacht building has somewhat declined at Cowes. Steamers have taken the place of sailing yachts where size is required, and the former are chiefly built in the North of England.

On the left the square tower of St. Mildred's, Whippingham, stands out among the trees, the park of Padmore slopes to the muddy banks, and Portland cement works perfume the air! On the right Parkhurst Forest, a royal forest, lies like a dark shadow on the horizon, and on its borders rise the red-brick buildings of the Albany Barracks, the Prison, and the Workhouse.

The miniature capital of the Wight has had a chequered history. Devastated more than once by the French and by the plague, it abounds also with later memories of the captive monarch of Carrisbrooke. In the Grammar School (the room is still to be seen) sat for three months the Commissioners arranging the Treaty of Newport with Charles I. He resided at the Grammar School, founded

1614, and the commissioners put up at the Bugle Inn. In St. Thomas's Church, lately restored, rests all that was mortal of the ill-fated Princess Elizabeth, who died at Carrisbrooke Castle, not two years after her father met his death at Whitehall. The Queen has erected a beautiful monument to her memory, by Marrochetti, with an effigy taken from a portrait in Her Majesty's possession, in white marble, representing the unhappy princess in the attitude in which she died, her cheek leaning on her father's Bible.

But a mile's walk from Newport, through the suburbs and up the steep chalk hill, takes the tourist to Carrisbrooke. The great Barbican gateway of Anthony Woodville, Lord of the Island (notice the white rose of York, surmounting the Woodville arms), is the glory of Carrisbrooke. On payment of a fee of 4d., the visitor explores the Governor's lodgings, Norman work of Baldwin de Redvers and his successors, the early Tudor buildings where Charles I. was confined, and ascends by a long flight of steps the mound on which stands the Norman keep. He is shown the room where the Princess Elizabeth died, the window where her ill-fated father stuck in his attempted escape; the famous well, sunk to replace that in the keep which failed, causing Baldwin de Redvers to surrender the castle to Stephen. He will walk along the smooth bowling green which Colonel Hammond made out of the ancient tilt-yard for the recreation of his royal prisoner, and where the latter's daughter contracted her fatal chill. Further, a perambulation of the walls, about a mile in circumference, will repay him with lovely views of bold down and wooded valley, set in a half-circle of sea.

CHAPTER VIII.

To Newtown.

SAILING DIRECTIONS.—On coming out of Cowes Harbour leave the red buoy on port off the Club landing stage. Steer for Egypt Point. Leave Gurnard Bay on port, then steer for Salt Mead, red buoy off the ledge of that name. Then steer for Hampstead Ledge Buoy, flat-topped, till opposite mid-channel Newtown estuary. Leave the beacon on port hand, till you come to the point on port hand. Anchor there afloat, at all tides, 200 or 300 yards from the East shore, abreast or a little inside the notice boards. Row up to Newtown at H.W., or to Clamerkin three or four miles at H.W.

Rounding Egypt Point to the west, the dip of Gurnard Bay comes into view, villa-crowned, and a sluggish stream ebbs into the Solent, over a shingle bank. Here is the traditional ford over to the Hampshire coast, at Lepe, where, according to Diodorus Seculus, the Phœnician tin-carts crossed to the great central tin-depôt at Niton, on the other side of the Island. Even up to Elizabeth's time the sea passage between Gurnard and Lepe was "the common passage of the isle." The name Rue, or route lingers in Rue Copse, Rue Common, King's Rue, in Hants; and in Rue Street, one of the roads through Parkhurst Forest, is a trace of one of the British or Roman roads southward, through the downs at Gatcombe, or the Gate Valley, to Puckaston Cove, where the Roman fleet lay.

The days of glory of Newtown, or Francheville, as it was then called, were in the reign of the second Edward, when the three days fair known as "Newtown Bandy," filled its long High Street and Gold Street with folk from all parts of the Island, and when it had a weekly market. But in 1377 the French landed, and utterly destroyed both Francheville and Yarmouth, occupying all the western part of the Island, and even attempting Carrisbrooke itself, where, however, they were cut up in an ambuscade. For two hundred years the little town on the Caul Bourn below the downs, lay desolate. In Elizabeth's reign it was rebuilt and incorporated, returning two members to Parliament up to 1832, when its electors numbered but nine. It is now a mere village; even its shipping and its oyster trade have deserted it. Gold Street is a mere waste, and the Town Hall, on an eminence overlooking the town, was turned into a school in 1832. The mayoral mace of the 15th century and the corporation seal are in the possession of Sir Barrington Simeon, of Swainston, hard by.

Among the members that this rotten little borough had the honour of returning was John, Duke of Marlborough, George Canning, and Admiral Sir Thomas Hopson. This latter was a tailor's apprentice of Niton, who ran away to sea, and joined the British fleet as it rounded St. Catharine's. He had the great good luck to come in the same day with the engagement, in which he distinguished himself by taking the French flag from the mainmast of the enemy's flagship. He made his way steadily up the ladder of promotion, distinguished himself in many fights, rose to be an admiral, and was knighted by Queen

Anne. To the extreme astonishment of his neighbours, who had believed him drowned at sea, Admiral " Snip," as he was nicknamed in allusion to his early calling, returned to his native isle, and sat in Parliament for the borough of Newtown.

From Newtown walks may be taken to Hamstead, a farmhouse designed by Nash, on high ground above the sea; and to Shalfleet, a pretty village in the thickly wooded lowland between the sea and the down, the remains of Watching-well, or Watching-wood, the earliest royal forest in England, enclosed by William I. The church of Shalfleet, Early English, is interesting, with square Norman tower and north door, and Purbeck nave columns.

> "The Shalfleet people, poor and simple,
> Sold the bells to build the steeple,"

and the gun belonging to the church too. The result is a wooden spire surmounting the large, thick Norman tower.

Ningwood is the nearest station of the Newport and Freshwater Railway. Beyond, up the valley of the Caul Bourne, lies Calbourne, one of the loveliest villages in the Island, in which are laid scenes in the "Silence of Dean Maitland." Behind, in the woods, Westover Manor (Moulton Barratt, Esq.). Beyond, again, a wild down country, Westover, Chillerton, and Blackdown Downs, some of the highest ground in the Island, and containing interesting remains of British villages. On Mottestone Down is a cromlech, the Longstone.

Swainston (Sir Barrington Simeon), on the Newport Road, in lovely grounds under the Downs, is on the site of the ancient palace of the Bishops of Winchester, of which there are but few remains.

CHAPTER IX.

To Yarmouth.

SAILING DIRECTIONS.—Steer out of Newtown on the Fairway Buoy. Clear Hampstead Ledge Buoy, leaving it to port. Then follow the coast-line, and make Yarmouth Pier. Yarmouth is well sheltered by the breakwater. A small harbour due is charged. Anchor at H.W. in seven feet of water off west side of pier; or inside breakwater afloat; or up river on mud. The best water is about twenty yards from head of pier to where vessels unload at head of quay. The channel is twenty yards wide. You cannot get in at lowest tides. You can row up the Yar to Freshwater Church with the tide.

Yarmouth is the headquarters of the Solent Yacht Club. Before the rise of Cowes, Yarmouth, or Eremouth, was the principal port of the Island, and was incorporated by Baldwin de Redvers. But it was devastated by the French in 1377, and again early in the sixteenth century, its church destroyed, and its bells carried off to Cherbourg, where they are still to be seen, with the inscription, "Eremue I. of W." Fortified by Henry VIII. and Elizabeth, Yarmouth began to look up again. The church was rebuilt, and Sir Robert Holmes, governor in the reign of Charles II., drained the marshes, and added to the fortifications. He built a stately mansion, now the George Inn, and still adorned with the royal coat of arms, a griffin, taken from the castle. Here he entertained the Merry Monarch, who presented the Corporation with a handsome mace, and held his hands over the iron rails, still existing at the back of the George, to be kissed by his loyal subjects. Later, "free trade" was the great employment in Yarmouth, as constant discoveries in old houses of secret recesses, movable hearthstones, etc., etc., still prove. In the church, the Holmes chapel, with the statue of Sir Robert, who took New York, and a handsome lectern and hour-glass are to be noticed.

At Yarmouth begin the chain of forts which girdle the western end of the Island and the peninsula formed by the Yar, which rises a few hundred feet from Freshwater Bay. On this side the Solent is practically hermetically sealed to an enemy's fleet. Yarmouth Harbour is an excellent centre from which to explore this peninsula, so varied in its character, such a contrast of bracing down and bosky valley, and where, at one spot, the sea may be heard to beat at once on both shores.

Freshwater is a gap in the great chalk southern rampart of the Island. Less than a century ago George Morland, the landscape painter, immortalized this coast when it was the haunt of the smuggler. The late laureate bought Farringford, under "the ridge of a noble down," in 1851, and made it his home till, during the summer months, he was driven away by the tripper and the tourist. Here he wrote "Maud" and the "Idylls," and described his new home in the following lines to his friend, the Rev. F. D. Maurice :—

"Where, far from smoke and noise of town,
  I watch the twilight falling brown,
  All round a careless ordered garden,
  Close to the ridge of a noble down.

> "Groves of pine on either hand,
> To break the blast of winter, stand;
> And further on, the hoary channel
> Tumbles and breaks on chalk and sand."

Here most of the noteworthy literary, political, and royal personages of the last half-century have visited him. Hidden by trees, the house stands back from the road, which skirts the park palings, on which gossip reputes the Yankee tourist was sitting with a telescope to spy upon the poet. The house is modern, but the summer-house is built upon Maiden Croft, the site of an ancient oratory to the Virgin. The faint odour of a legend clings about the place, that of a submarine passage to France, beginning under the down behind the house, and stored with treasure, dragon-guarded.

From Freshwater a walk may be taken East over Afton Down, to Brooke (Colonel Seeley, M.P.), noticing the tumuli and the obelisk to a child who fell over the cliff. West, over High Down 490 feet, to the Needles Fort, with perpendicular chalk cliffs 400 feet high on the left all the way, and a glorious view of the Freshwater Peninsula below, of the dark New Forest across the strip of Solent, of the Dorset coast curving away to Poole, and the peninsula of Purbeck, with the Old Harry Point, the counterpart of the Needles, thirteen miles away, opposite.

Scratchell's Bay is South of the Needles. The headland is crowned by a fort. Beyond lie the famous chalk masses. From the fort a path leads down to Alum Bay with its queer-coloured geological strata, contrasting so strangely with the stern, bare grandeur of the southern cliffs.

When the tide admits, the sands can be taken all the way back to Yarmouth firm and dry. Otherwise the walk is up Headon Hill, through Totland, by Warden Point,

Colville Bay, by gorse-clad chines, with lovely views of sea, meadow and valley. Near Warden Point are the galleries of the elaborate range-finding mechanism which communicates with Hurst Castle, hermetically sealing this entrance to the Solent. At Cliff End Fort, Hurst is but 1,460 yards away. At Sconce Point is Victoria Fort, originally fortified in Elizabeth's reign.

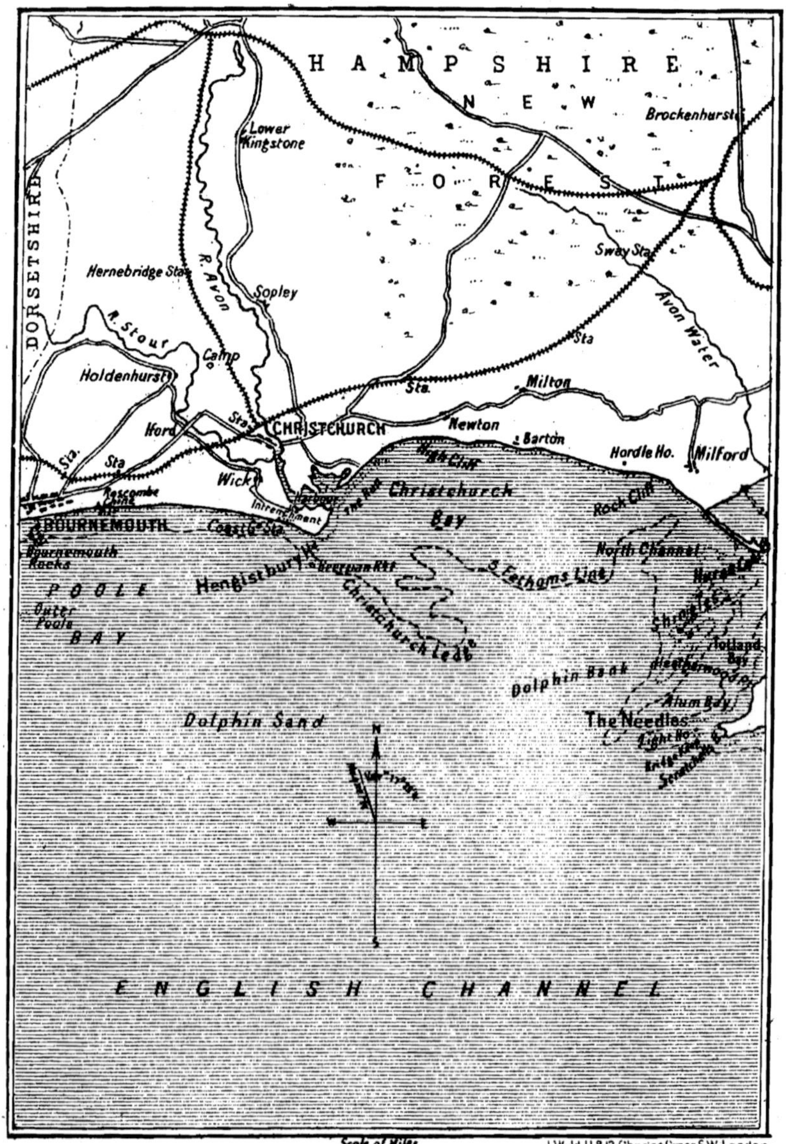

Scale of Miles

0 1 2 3 4 5

J. Wyld, 11 & 12, Charing Cross S.W. London.

CHAPTER X.

Round and about the Needles.

SAILING DIRECTIONS.—To Alum Bay going out of Yarmouth at H.W. go outside the Black Rock Buoy at L.W.; inside at H. But close inside the buoy is rock, so give it a wide berth. Steer for Sconce Fort, then for Warden Ledge Buoy; then steer in West of Totland Bay Pier, and anchor 200 yards outside to West. There is nice lying, sheltered from all winds W. to S.E. Land on pier or at H.W. on sand.

Some of the walks described in preceding chapter may be taken from Alum Bay.

Sailing Directions.—A day cruise, wind permitting, may be taken to the Needles and Freshwater Gate on the South coast of the Island in *fine* weather. It should only be attempted when wind is N.E. to N.N.W., *never* when fresh wind from S.W. to S.E. In strong winds dangerous puffs blow off from E. and S.E. and strike in all directions from the land.

To Alum Bay.—Give Heatherwood Point a wide berth till Alum Pier is open, as there are outlying rocks West of it. You can lie for the night at Alum Bay, sheltered from S.W. to S.E. winds.

To the Needles.—Sail to the Needles Lighthouse, giving a berth of 50 yards unless dead low water, because of a flat rock, when give 150 yards. Steer clear of Sun Corner till Freshwater Gate opens, giving the coast a berth of 200 or 300 yards because of a few outlying rocks. Anchor for two or three hours in Freshwater Bay, with a sandy bottom in the middle of the bay.

To the Needles, rowing.—Through the Needles Rocks, and Scratchell's Bay to Sun Corner, and land on the beach there.

Totland Bay is a fast-rising watering-place, where supplies can be obtained. At Alum Bay is the Needles Hotel. From either point day cruises may be made round the Needles to Freshwater, or in the dinghey in through Needles Rocks to Scratchell's Bay. The whole coast is magnificent and full of natural wonders of cave and arch and rock, and presenting surprising spectacles and contrasts. The wonderful variegated strata of Alum Bay, forming a wall nearly a quarter of a mile in length, and 400 feet in height, resembling, geologically, Whitecliff Bay at the other extremity of the Island, are best seen from the sea. To it abruptly succeeds the white headland of the Needles, with its celebrated line of detached chalk masses. The former Needles Lighthouse stood on the North Point, 474 feet above the sea. The present one is on the most western of the pinnacles, nearer the water, where it is in less danger of being concealed by fog. It contains a revolving red and white light, visible ten miles out at sea, and a fog bell audible at five miles' distance.

Scratchell's Bay is a lofty curve of towering white precipices. Near the Needles, the Needles Cave runs 300 feet into the cliff. Landing on the strip of shingle beach below this stupendous line, the tourist can fully appreciate the grandeur of the scene, and view the magnificent natural arch, 3C0 feet high, forming an alcove, which overhangs this beach 150 feet.

TO THE SOLENT AND POOLE HARBOUR. 59

Rounding Sun Corner, the line of cliffs known as Main Bench, 617 feet high, comes into view. It is the West portion of the glittering wall of Freshwater Cliffs, which extend for three miles from Freshwater Gate to the Sun Corner, and during the summer months is the home of thousands of sea birds. Among the wonderful caves, arches, which have been worn in the cliff by the action of the sea, and which are passed in succession as follows :— The Wedge Rock, fixed between a detached pillar and the cliff; Old Pepper Rock, Roe Hall, 600 feet high. Lord Holmes' Parlour, where a former Warden of the Island is said to have entertained his guests; Lord Holmes' Cellar. Frenchman's Hole, where a fugitive French prisoner was starved to death. Bar Cave, 90 feet deep. Neptune's Caves, the larger 200 feet deep, and many others. At the East end of Freshwater Bay is the Arched Rock, natural Gothic. Close to it is the Deer Pond, another chalk mass, and beyond in Afton Cliff are several caves.

CHAPTER XI.

To Swanage.

SAILING DIRECTIONS.—From the Needles to Swanage Bay. Course, W. ¾ N., distance about 13½ miles.

Swanage is sheltered from W. to N.E. winds. But there is often a nasty swell which makes it an unpleasant anchorage. Lie off the pier in 2 fathoms, about ¾ of a mile off shore. Sandy bottom.

Swanage is a good shelter against West winds. Since the opening of the railway from Wareham it has fast risen into a watering-place, and villas and lodging-houses straggle up the downs behind the little stone-roofed town, and bathing-machines jostle the heaps of cut stone lying ready for shipment on the beach. The picturesque corner of the South-West coast, known as the Isle or Peninsula of Purbeck, has been opened up by land. To the water traveller it is easily explored from Swanage. Nowhere, probably, within so small an area is there such variety of scenery. The diversified strata along the coast from Old Harry Point to St. Alban's Head are well known to geologists, and of necessity vary the landscape on the surface. A wild tract of moorland waste, sparsely populated, poorly roaded, alternately, according to the season, golden with gorse, purple with the heather, and shadowed with fir woods, is intersected with the winding creeks and bays of far-spreading Poole Harbour. The bold chalk range of the Purbeck Hills, rising at Nine Barrow Down to the height of seven hundred feet, bisects the peninsula. Many a forgotten hero of pre-historic ages sleeps under the tumuli which give their names to the different summits. Where, at the nick on the downs Corfe Castle still proudly rears its ruined head, the stone country begins, and extends to the iron-bound coast of sheer dark rock which extends to the magnificent cape of St. Alban's, broken here and there by picturesque coves, such as Warbarrow and Kimmeridge Bay, Lulworth Cove, Chapman's Pool. Many has been the wreck on those merciless precipices when the wild sou'-westers rage up channel.

Swanage lies snugly on the western horn of a white bay facing the east between Peverel and Ballard Heads. There is a lighthouse on the former, and a little pier juts into the bay, used chiefly for lading the stone lighters with the staple product of the district, familiar to all in kerbstones and street pavements in London. Lobsters are a speciality of Swanage. The Isle of Purbeck Yacht Club have their headquarters at Swanage. Messrs. Burt & Mowlem, stone merchants, are the local magnates and good genii. The church has been "restored," but there are sundry fine specimens of ancient domestic architecture within a walk. Newtown Manor is the residence of Sir Charles Robinson, a well-known antiquarian. In his curio-hunting travels all over Europe in connection with the South Kensington Museum, he has garnered rich spoil in the old Purbeck Manor House, standing back from the road amid fine old elms and trim gardens. The huge manorial barn (and "Darset" is famous for its barns;

witness the local proverb, "as big as a parson's barn") has been transformed into a dining-hall, with a mullion window where the great door stood, and a carved Florentine stone mantel-piece, and brass fire-back and dogs. Ancient leather chairs from Portugal, and old French tapestry, furnish the room. Whitecliff, an old farmhouse, supposed to have been the residence of King John, lies 1½ miles to the North, and Godlingston, formerly a monastery, with very ancient remains, 1½ miles to the Northwest.

Along the cliffs and downs to the South are the various stone quarries which have been worked for nearly 700 years, for the Purbeck marble forms the top layer of the strata in which the geologist finds so much to interest him. The "Swanage crocodile," now in the British Museum, was discovered here in 1847. Tilly Whim is one of the most ancient and remarkable of the quarries, cut out of the sheer face of the black cliff into Cyclopean chambers like some old Egyptian rock temple. The Dancing Ledge, a peculiar shelving beach of rock; Connaught's Hole, a wonderful natural arch, are some of the sights of this interesting strip of coast, which runs past Seacombe Valley, where the East Indiaman *Halsewell* was wrecked, and where the victims lie buried in the grassy nick between the cliffs, to St. Alban's Head. A curious tiny Norman chapel, used as a beacon in former days, but now restored by Lord Eldon, and used in summer mornings for service, crowns the famous headland. It is lighted by one slit window, and the door is worth noticing. A little hole in the central pillar, which forms the roof, was used as a wishing place by local young people, who, crooking a pin and dropping it in the hole, muttered the wish they hoped might come true. To the

West below lies Lord Eldon's seat of Encombe in the valley of the Golden Bowl, and South beneath the cape, even on the calmest summer's day, swirls the dreaded St. Alban's Race, caused by the confluence of currents.

CHAPTER XII.

To Studland.

SAILING DIRECTIONS.—From Swanage follow coast-line to Old Harry Rock or Handfast Point; give these ¼ mile berth in rounding. Anchor between the Red Cliff and Old Harry in 1½ fathoms.

Studland is better sheltered from West winds than Swanage, but is much exposed to E. and S.E. winds when a nasty swell gets up. So it can only be recommended for a few hours' stay.

Studland, embosomed in tall elms, and sheltered by the downs, lies just above the Red Cliff, a jutting mass of sandstone where at the bottom of the bay the chalk precipice meets the rolling country of moor and pinewood, of sand dune, mere, and winding creek. The bay is shoaly, covered with masses of floating seaweed, and the shelving beach not unsuspected of treacherous quicksands, where lives have been lost. A steep gully, feathery with the *osmunda regalis*, leads up to the village, where from thatched stone cottages in deep lanes emerge sun-bonneted, fair-haired women, with the Saxon eyes of Dorset, speaking in the soft Wessex twang, with " a's " for " o's," and " v's " for " f's." It is the ideal village of a story book. But one public-house, and not a lodging to be let. Such is the stern decree of the landowner, Mr. Bankes, of Corfe Castle. At the cross-road are the scanty remains of a stone cross, and through the trees to the left the gables of the Manor House rise against the blue sea and white cliffs beyond. On the right a path leads across a field to the glory of Studland, a tiny Norman church, comparatively little known, but the rival of Stukely and Iffley. The never-finished central tower rises among the tall elms and cypresses. It contains a bell with a date anterior to the Conquest, and the legend inscribed: "Draw neare to God." The interior is dark and severe, the massive tower dividing the nave and chancel, which is lighted by a fine Early English triplet window, and contains an altar tomb of the 15th century. In the nave is an ancient font, and a south window has been inserted, of painted glass, to the memory of Major Bankes, who perished in the Mutiny. But his truer memorials are the ruins of Bankes' Bungalow and Bankes' Battery in the Lucknow Residency, which he so nobly defended. Like so many seaside churches, the dedication is to St. Nicholas, and in the churchyard lie not a few strangers, the "harvest of the sea." Close to the door sleeps an old Peninsula hero, a native of Studland, and the late landlord of the village ale-house, to which he brought back fourteen clasps, the Waterloo medal, and an old wound from the forlorn hope at Badajoz. Besides him lies his French wife he wooed and won during the occupation of Paris in the winter before Waterloo.

An atmosphere of Satanic legend pervades this secluded country. At the Old Harry Rocks on Handfast Point, Ballard Down comes to an abrupt end in the sea, facing its counterpart, the Needles, fifteen miles away. Walking over the down, one looks down on these two huge chalk pillars, Old Harry and his wife, standing in the sea. Round the point from the slippery slopes, where the

F

sheep graze dizzily, and the sea-gulls wing up from sea-green coves below, the geologist will peer over the sheer white wall, and note the remarkable " fault " in the strata, and the huge cavern called the " Parson's Barn." In the opposite direction, towards the North across the purple moor on a knoll, lies the Devil's Nightcap, or Agglestone, Anglo-Saxon *hælig stone*, an erratic block of ferruginous sandstone, shaped like an inverted cone, sixteen feet high by thirty-six feet round and sixteen in diameter, weighing 400 tons. The legend goes that the Prince of Evil seated one day on the Needles threw his night-cap at Corfe Castle, then building, and that it fell short and turned into the Agglestone. The artificial morass which surrounds the boulder, as well as excavations on its surface, prove it to have been connected with heathen worship.

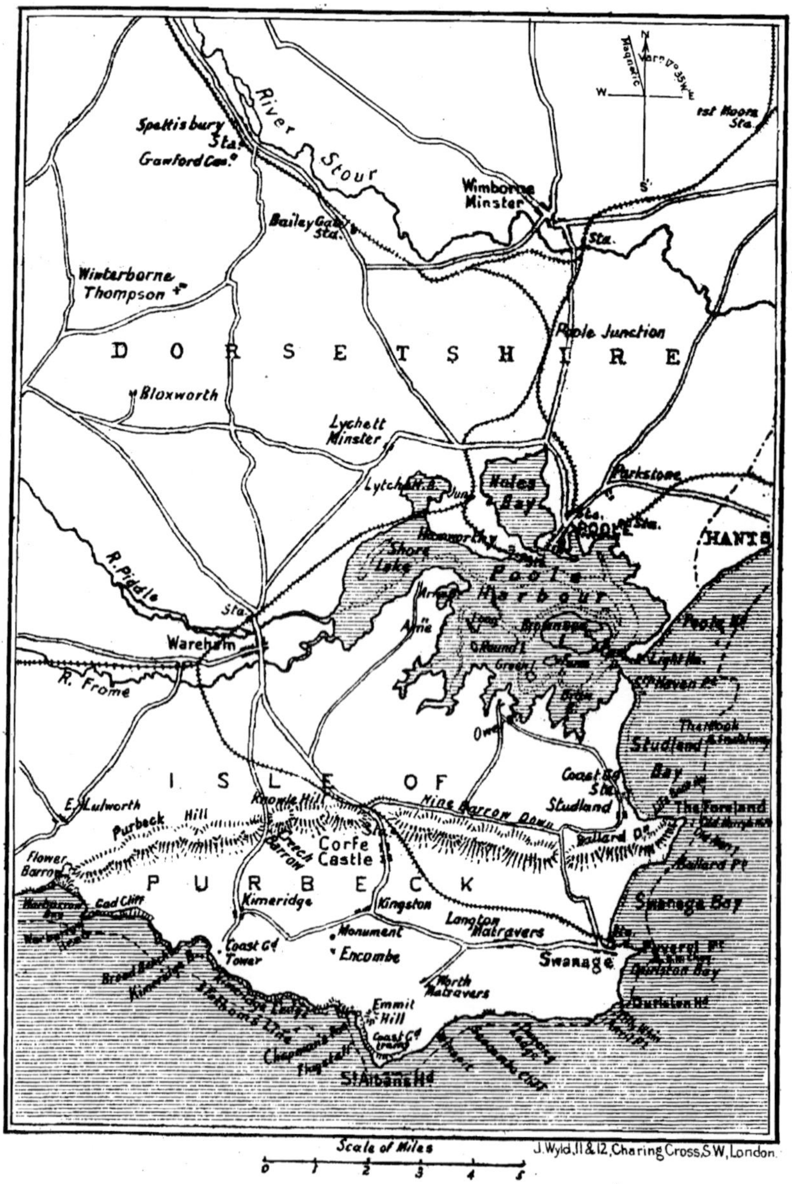

J. Wyld, 11 & 12, Charing Cross, S.W., London.

CHAPTER XIII.

Up Poole Harbour.

SAILING DIRECTIONS.—Steer in from the offing with the Lighthouses on North Haven Point in line, which will lead over the Bar in not less than nine feet of water. Leave the red and white buoys to port, and the black buoys to starboard on entering. When past the inner red buoy, be careful not to make too bold with the West side. The East side is steep to; keep about one cable off it, and do not turn too sharp round the North-West angle of East side of entrance.

Either anchor under Branksea Island with the bell buoy (red and white) bearing from East round to South, or proceed to Poole.

At night keep the lights in line crossing Bar. When over Bar, keep high light, its apparent breadth open to East of low light, till the land at North Haven is seen, when give it a berth of one cable and anchor in Branksea Road till daylight.

You can anchor in South Deep between Harry Point on the Island and Stone Island; or in Whitley Lake below Parkstone Quay; but though this is staked it requires local knowledge to find. Supplies cannot be obtained nearer than Poole or Parkstone.

To Poole, about $2\frac{1}{2}$ miles.—Leave Bell Buoy and all parti-coloured buoys to port, and black beacons with barrels on them to starboard.

Anchor to West of red and white buoy at entrance to Poole Creek in about three fathoms at L.W.

To Wareham.—Channel beaconed. Anchor off Hamworthy Clay Works Pier, or Russell Quay. Hence row up to Swineshead Point, which is within a mile of Wareham, walking across the marshes.

To Wych, for Corfe Castle.—A very devious and intricate channel, requiring local assistance. The Channel runs round the North and West of Branksea Island, and then to Shifstal Point, below Arne encampment (170 feet high). Then due South past Long and Round Island. Below this anchor in Wych Lake, and row up to Ferry opposite Wych Farm, where the Corfe brook runs down a wooded glen into the harbour, and walk up this and strike across the heath to Corfe Castle.

To Goathorn Point Hard; Redhorn Quay and Ower Lake. Up the South Deep opposite North Haven. The channel is staked. Row to Greenland Pier from Redhorn. Anchor in Ower Lake beyond Green Island, and row to hard at Ower passage.

Poole Harbour is a magnificent estuary 40 miles in circumference, but owing to its shallowness and the devious channels among the lakes or creeks, requires knowing. When a little local knowledge has been obtained, however, the yachtsman in a craft drawing but some 6 feet of water, will be well rewarded by sails in smooth water whatever the weather may be in the open sea outside the Sandhead Spit, and by charming walks ashore among wooded glens, over heathery heaths, and on lonely islets.

The southern landing-place of Branksea or Brownsey

TO THE SOLENT AND POOLE HARBOUR. 69

Island is at what the late owner, Mr. George Cavendish-Bentinck, a well-known art collector, who showered upon his island home all sorts of antiquarian treasures from foreign parts, designated as the Piazza di Castello. And, indeed, the quiet waters, the pine trees feathering the shore, the turrets and loggia, the bathing steps and terraces of the castle, washed by the incoming tide, give the spot quite a foreign air. Mediæval fountains, antique statues, great stone washing basins from some disused monastery, tablets, capitals of columns, fragments of carving, are scattered everywhere. Upon them all looks down the square Tudor keep, a patch of warm red-brick colour backed by the pine woods.

On Branksea Island, in the reign of Henry II., the abbot of Cerne, in Dorset, built a chapel and a hermitage; and the right of wreckage, in those days considered a lawful perquisite, was granted to Cerne. Canute landed here in 1015. Queen Elizabeth gave the castle and island to her favourite, Sir Christopher Hatton, of terpsichorean fame. There was much jealousy between the Governor and the Mayor of Poole respecting the dues payable by ships entering the harbour. The vessel naturally objected to pay twice, and Sir Christopher demanded his due at the harbour mouth,—the Mayor, at Poole Quay. Into one recalcitrant brig the Governor fired a broadside from the battery of six cannon, marked with the royal rose, which still lie rusting under the pines on the sandcliff facing the entrance. The vessel sank, and Sir Christopher received a reprimand from his mistress and was dismissed.

In 1852, Col. Waugh, a distinguished Indian officer, bought the island. He faced the stern red brick with pseudo-Gothic mullions, oriels, turrets, and lancets, in white stone, and embellished the interior with dark panelling, oak stairs and balustrades. He erected upon a knoll a church, which has been adorned by Mr. Bentinck with a Florentine font, Venetian candelabra, and a Murillo in the baptistery under the tower. He reclaimed some hundred acres of land, built clusters of cottages in various parts, and discovered the valuable china clay pits. Unfortunately, before all his improvements were completed, this clay was found on the mainland also, whence transport was cheaper, and Col. Waugh became insolvent, and the very name of Branksea Island an evil echo to the minds of the many who were dragged down in his ruin. Mr. Bentinck has restored and completed the castle, from the flat roof of which is a fine view—from the Needles to the Dorset Downs, and of the harbour.

Though the island is private property, it is possible to obtain permit to land and inspect it. Branksea is some five miles in circumference, and charming is a walk round the edge, under the pines, across the heather, along the sandcliffs, past the lonely mere called the decoy-pond, back again to the battery point and the trim terraces, and the winter gardens round the Castle.

Poole.

Like a Venice of the North, the ancient seaport of Poole stands on a promontory amid lagoons at the head of the winding channel, creeks and "lakes" of the vast haven which bears its name, a haven equal in size to that of Milford, and which would be useful as a harbour of refuge for battle ships, were it but deeper. The town, chiefly of red brick, reminds one somewhat of Sheerness and old Portsmouth. The High Street, nearly a mile long, runs down to a line of quays. Its principal trade is pottery clay and timber from Norway. It contains little to interest the antiquarian. The Town Hall is a renaissance building in the High Street; there are some fine old mansions, formerly the residences of the Newfoundland Company Merchants, in the thriving days of that trade some century back, as is shown by arms of the Company, codfish crossed, which are carved on the marble mantel-pieces. On the Wool Quay is the ancient chapel of the Holy Spirit, now used as a storehouse. A gateway of the date of Richard III. is to be seen. Poole is mentioned in the reign of Henry III. It furnished four ships and ninety-four men to the siege of Calais under Edward. It was ravaged by the "Black Death" in 1349, and the victims interred on a tongue of land known as the "Baiter." When Henry VII., as Earl of Richmond, was endeavouring to raise the West, he stood off Poole, but did not effect a landing. The importance of the place fell off in the reign of Henry VIII., for Leland speaks of it as a "poore fisshar village." It revived during the Civil Wars, when Poole espoused staunchly the Parliamentary cause, in spite of being summoned by the Marquis of Hertford. A long series of retaliations between the seaport and the neighbouring castle of Corfe marked the next few years. The men of Poole caught troops of Prince Rupert's, and relieved them of £3,000. Twice they besieged Corfe Castle. Prince Maurice attempted to attack the town in 1643. The following month the townsfolk decoyed a force of the Earl of Crawford, defeating it badly. In 1644, however, Sir Thomas Anson drove a troop of Parliamentary horse into the very port of Poole, laughing at the cannon-balls from the walls. In October the governor retaliated by capturing forty of the royal horse and two colours.

Poole has often been honoured by Royal visits. King John embarked and disembarked here more than once. Charles II. stopped here in 1665, on his way from London to Salisbury, to escape the plague. Charles X. of France landed here after his abdication. Poole has had an unenviable notoriety as a hotbed of smuggling, and the headquarters of privateering. The former was only put down after a desperate resistance, and some of the Poole buccaneers are famous in history. Notably, Harry Page, or Arripay, who harassed France and Spain. He "scoured the channel of Flanders so powerfully that no ship could pass that way without being taken." He brought in at one time one hundred and twenty prizes from Brittany, took the crucifix off Cape Finisterre, and ravaged the coast of Spain in 1406. The kings of France and Spain fitted out an expedition against him, under the Count of Buelna, and a battle took place at Poole, in which Arripay's brother was killed. In 1694 Jolliffe, the master of a small Poole hoy, attacked a French privateer three times his size, which had captured an English fishing boat, and drove her ashore at Lulworth, for which feat he received a gold medal and chain from William III. The next year Thompson, the master of a small fishing vessel, with a man and boy, took a French privateer of Cherbourg, with sixteen men, and brought her into Poole, receiving a gold medal from the Admiralty. In 1794, when a Poole brig had been captured by the French, the mate, one man, and a boy rose and recaptured it, taking it into Cork. An old doggerel thus reflects on the daring and morality of the inhabitants:—

"If Poole was a fish-pool, the men of Poole fish,
There'd be a pool for the devil, and fish for his dish."

Wimborne.

Wimborne is such a short run by train from Poole, over a heathery waste, that a visit there should not be neglected, on account of its beautiful minster. Upton House, famous in the Tichborne trial, is passed on the left, the park lying across the lagoon. Wimborne Minster was founded in 1043 by Edward the Confessor, on the site of the collegiate church of Cuthberga, sister of King Ina, founded 700, and destroyed by the Danes 978. It is a magnificent cruciform erection, unequalled for its size in severe beauty, with a red sandstone North central tower, and a perpendicular tower at the West end. The two-storied lantern, with triforium and clerestory, is especially fine. The glory of the building is the choir, Norman and Early English; the east window very beautiful. The choir contains the altar-tomb, with alabaster effigies of John Beaufort, Duke of Somerset, and his wife; and a floor-slab of Purbeck marble to King Ethelred, brother of Alfred the Great. The north transept is known as the "Death's" Aisle, from a former fresco on the walls. An orrery at the West end should be noticed, also brass eagle lectern, presented 1623. The church records, contained in several fine old chests, date from 1475. Over a decorated sacristy is a perpendicular library, with two hundred and forty-three valuable volumes, some chained. One of them—Sir Walter Raleigh's "History of the World"—has a hole burnt in it by Matthew Prior, the poet, who, when a boy, used to pore over the books by the light of a candle stuck in a bit of wood. The library was presented to the town in 1614. The gems are a Black Letter Bible, 1595, and a MS. dated 1343.

Wareham.

Wareham is a most ancient town, mentioned in the *Anglo-*

Saxon Chronicle; but the quadrangular earthworks, which the now shrunken town does not fill, are of older origin, probably British. It was attacked and devastated by the Danes under Canute. In the wars between Stephen and Matilda, Wareham suffered much, being burnt by the former, and then besieged by the forces of the latter. Prince Henry shipped hence to Anjou when driven out by Stephen, and King John twice landed here. The strength of its position caused Wareham to become a bone of contention in the Civil Wars. It declared for the king, and its character for "dreadful malignancy" was the cause of its entire destruction by Sir Astley Cooper. In the last century it was again destroyed by fire. There are scanty remains of a Priory founded in 709 by Aldhelm, Bishop of Sherborne. Castle Hill was the site of a Norman stronghold. "Bloody Bank," on the West side of the walls, was the scene of the execution of Monmouth's adherents by Judge Jefferies. S. Mary's Church is the only one in use of some half-dozen churches which formerly existed, and of which two others yet remain, and is very ancient. The chapel in the south aisle is said to be the resting-place of Saxon kings, and in it was at first buried Edmund the Martyr, after his murder at Corfe. It is a double-storied chapel, very singular. An 11th century leaden font, with carved figures of the twelve apostles, is worth notice; also inscriptions on East end of north aisle, supposed to refer to Calway, an Armorican bishop who visited Britain about 430.

From Wareham the train may be taken to Wool, the next station, whence a walk of one and a half miles to Bindon Abbey, a Cistercian foundation of 1172, lying pleasantly among brooks and trees. The ground-plan may be traced, and there are fragments of the church, the two western towers, a solid screen, two side altars, monumental slabs, and the foundations of the domestic offices. There was formerly a peal of twelve bells, but local doggerel runs :—

"Wool streams and Combewells,
Fordington cuckolds stole Bindon bells,"

and they are now in these three neighbouring churches.

Wool Church is Early English, with a curious pulpit cloth of velvet, part of an old cope. Close to the bridge is an old manor-house, now a farmhouse, with a barn on an 11th century basement.

From Wool a pleasant walk of about three miles along foot-paths across the fields leads to Lulworth Castle, the seat of the Weld family since 1650, surrounded by a park five miles in circumference, and lying in a most secluded locality. To the East for ten miles stretch a waste of moors, down to Poole Harbour; South the range of chalk downs reach to the coast. The castle was built about 1600, out of the ruins of Bindon Abbey. It is a square structure, with a tower at each corner, containing a state bedroom once occupied by Charles X. of France, and some fine pictures. In the Civil Wars it was held for the king by Lord Bindon, and the Parliamentarians committed some havoc in 1644. James I., Charles II, and George III. have been entertained at Lulworth.

A walk over Bindon Hill, or Swinesback Hill, leads to West Lulworth and its famous cove. The cliffs are of geological interest. The cove itself is a curious circular basin, worn into the chalk, with caves and rocks. West Lulworth is fast rising into a little watering-place. Above the cove stands a little unused Early English chapel.

Corfe Castle is easiest reached from Poole Harbour

from Wych, two and a half miles' walk, or from Ower, four miles.

Ower was once the port of Purbeck, shipping much stone and marble. It was also the scene of quaint customs on Marblers' Day, the annual festival of the Purbeck quarrymen, who used to form a guild, to which birth was the only admittance. After the holding of the Marblers' Court at Corfe borough, the quarrymen marched in procession down to Ower, enjoying the prerogative of kissing every unmarried woman they met. At Ower Point they played a game of football, the football being presented by the last married quarryman.

Corfe.

The marblers' little stone-roofed town nestles picturesquely under the ruins of its noble castle. It has been a borough since Elizabeth; but its trade in stone and dark grey marble has now deserted it to a great extent, and the chief industry of the neighbourhood is in digging for potter's clay, largely used in Minton's china works. The church has been rebuilt, with the exception of the tower; but the font is very beautiful and ancient. There is a fine old mansion of the Dackhams, with carved oak.

The name Corfe is derived from the Anglo-Saxon *ceorfan*, to cut, designating the nick in the downs in which the castle is reared, a landmark for miles across down and moor. It was the hunting lodge of Queen Elfrida in the forest of Purbeck, and here she murdered her stepson, Edward, by stabbing him in the back as he sat in the gateway on his horse, drinking a cup she tendered him on his return from the chase. Legend says the horse dragged the murdered king's body down to the brook below the castle. There it lay till carried off for burial at Wareham, where a leaden sarcophagus has been recently discovered which probably held it, and whence it was translated, uncorrupt, to Shaftesbury.

The castle of Corfe is first mentioned in the reign of Henry II. But the keep was built by William I. Corfe was at once the Windsor and the state prison of the Plantagenet kings, situated as it was in a happy hunting ground. Stephen attacked the castle in vain when held by Maud. John made it his favourite place of residence, and kept his regalia and treasure there. At Corfe he immured in a life-long captivity the Princess Eleanor, sister of his murdered nephew, Arthur of Brittany, in company with the two daughters of the Scottish king, sent as hostages. Here he also starved to death two hundred nobles of Anjou, imprisoned for complicity in a rising in aid of Arthur. The barons held Corfe for five years against Henry III., and Edward II. was imprisoned in the fortress prior to his murder at Berkeley. Elizabeth presented it to her favourite, Sir Christopher Hatton, from whom it passed to Lord Chief Justice Sir John Bankes, whose family, now residing at Kingston Lacy, near Wimborne, still own it and the surrounding country. In 1643 Sir John joined the king at York, and Lady Bankes was surprised by the Parliamentarians, under the guise of a May-day stag-hunt. She instantly caused the gates to be closed, summoned her few retainers, and, with the aid of her daughters, herself fired a cannon upon the enemy. But being unable to hold out, she feigned surrender, and, upon the advance of Prince Maurice, the besiegers retired. At the end of June, however, they invested the castle in force, captured the town from the adjacent downs, and, armed with two engines called the Sow and the Boar, proceeded to batter the castle, stripping the lead from the church roof to make ammunition. But if the assault was fierce, the defence was stubborn. The heroic *chatelaine* caused showers of stones, hot liquor, and burning embers to be poured down upon the assailants, who withdrew as help approached. In 1645 came the second siege, and Corfe succumbed to treachery, an officer of the garrison, Colonel Pitman, admitting the enemy in disguise. By order of the Parliament, Corfe was blown up. Never was a more terrible destruction. Yet it is incomplete, and the blocks of Cyclopean masonry, shattered and dislodged, still hang together in stupendous masses upon the impregnable position. The key and seal of Corfe Castle are at Kingston Lacy.

Encircled by two banks, the mound rises sheer on the East, West and North sides. Towards the town it is protected by a deep trench. The principal remains are the Queen's Tower, the Norman keep, the Horse-Shoe Tower, the Plukenet Tower (named after one of the constables of Corfe whose shield it bears), the Glorietta Bastion, and the Great Gateway. A bridge of four arches leads over the moat, protected by two round towers built by Sir Christopher Hatton, to the Great Gateway. An odd way of working portcullises, something on the lines of a modern sash window, should here be noticed. Another gateway, also *temp.* Edward I., leads from the outer to the second ward. It has been much injured, the left-hand tower having been moved bodily down hill some nine feet by the force of the explosion. Between the Buttevant octagonal tower on the West angle, and the tower in the middle of the curtain of the lower ward, are three plain herring-bone windows, probably fragments of Elfrida's Anglo-Saxon palace. In the middle ward, on the top of the hill, stands the Norman square keep and the Queen's Tower

(Henry III.) with the hall and chapel and castle well.

At Church Knole, one mile and a half, is the Edwardian manor-house of Barneston, with oak-roofed hall.

From Corfe walks may be taken East over Nine Barrow Down, 642 feet above the sea, towards Studland and the Agglestone, commanding one of the finest views in the country of purple moor and still loch, green down and blue sea, reminding one of Scotland. Or West, along Creech Barrow Down, 369 feet, with one of the most glorious prospects in the West of England, from Lulworth to the Needles. The seat of the Bonds, Creech Grange, a Tudor mansion, lies below Creech Barrow. An ancestor of the family built Bond Street, London, " to his great undoing."

CHAPTER XIV.

To Bournemouth, Christchurch, Hurst Castle, and Lymington.

SAILING DIRECTIONS.—Come out of Poole by the main channel as you went in. There is a narrow passage between the Hook Sands and North Haven, best not attempted without local knowledge. Steer for Bournemouth Pier, where you can lie for a few hours on East side sheltered from West wind.

To Christchurch.—Steer for buoy off Christchurch Ledge, which runs out under Hengistbury Head, black and white chequered. The day should be picked, and a wind E. to N. E. chosen. The course from Christchurch Ledge Buoy to the anchorage is N. by E. $\frac{3}{4}$ E., distance about $1\frac{1}{4}$ miles. The anchorage is in $1\frac{1}{2}$ fathoms, sheltered from E. and N.E. winds. From thence row ashore to coastguard station or fishing cottages, and get a local man to take you in, as the channel is much silted up, and very difficult to find, and only suitable for quite small-class boats.

Bournemouth, with its yellow sandcliffs, where the pine woods meet the sea, its Riviera-like appearance, and its acres of beautiful villas, each in their own pine-covered gardens, is well worth a passing visit, though there is nothing in it of historical interest to detain the sight-seer. Its great dryness, as well as the sheltered climate of its chines, place it in the first rank, if not indeed in the foremost position, among our health resorts. The neighbourhood is a charming one of heathery moor, fir wood, rhododendron-clad combe and glen : a bit of Scotland set down on the balmy South coast. Every attraction that a high-class watering-place can offer is possessed by Bournemouth.

Christchurch is mentioned in the *Anglo-Saxon Chronicle* in 900 as having been captured by Edward the Elder in his wars with his kinsman Ethelwald. Stowe tells us that Hengist, the Saxon invader, landed for his second invasion of England at Hengistbury Head, the bluff overlooking Christchurch Harbour, about a mile from the town, where a fosse and earthworks may still be traced. In the reign of Henry I., Baldwin de Redvers, Earl of Devon, who founded Quarr Abbey, the son-in-law of the Conqueror, built the castle upon an artificial mound. The massive walls still remain, ten feet thick.

The glorious Priory Church itself, pleasantly situated in the meadows close to the junction of the Stour and Avon, of salmon fame, is so old that no records remain of its foundation. It is supposed, according to Camden, to have been built in early Saxon times on the site of a heathen temple. William Rufus gave it to Flambard, Bishop of Durham, who practically rebuilt and enlarged it in 1075. From him it passed to Baldwin de Redvers. The huge and severe nave, with its double row of massive square pillars, is considered the finest specimen of Norman work in the kingdom. The choir is later; the grotesque carvings of the stalls there should be noticed. The magnificent ancient stone altar-piece, richly carved, represents the root and stem of Jesse. The Lady Chapel was built by Lady Alice West in 1398. Christchurch Priory is full of interesting tombs and effigies.; one to Margaret de la Pole, Countess of Salisbury, 1541 ; others by Flaxman, Chantrey, and notably that of the drowned poet Shelley, an exquisitely pathetic representation in white marble, erected by his son, Sir Percy Shelley, of Boscombe, near Bournemouth.

Sailing Directions.—From Christchurch, steer on Hurst Castle, giving the beach a fair berth. Take the North channel. The tide runs very strong. Lie in the Camber, North of the Castle, just afloat in mid-stream, or go up on H.W. to Quay Haven and ground.

To Lymington.—Steer for Lymington Spit Buoy, red and white chequered, passing with a small boat just inside it, and open out Jack in the Basket, a black boom, where there is good and safe anchorage. The river is beaconed all the way up. Lie afloat opposite the baths, and row up to the town ; or lie afloat at Inman's shipbuilding yard in one fathom.

Should it not be convenient to lie and land at Hurst Castle, the fortress may be reached from Lymington by a three-mile walk along the sea wall to Keyhaven Creek when the tide is up; otherwise the shingle is bad walking. Thence a boat may be taken to Hurst Castle. It stands at the extreme end of a wonderful shingle beach like the Chesil Beach, in Portland. It was one of Henry VIII.'s castles, one of his attempts to fortify the Solent and Portsmouth, and was built out of the ruins of Beaulieu Abbey. It consists of a circular tower, containing two barrack-rooms round a circular and winding staircase. On either side are granite walls 1,500 feet long. The castle is connected with the mainland and with London by telegraph, and also with the range-finding galleries on the opposite coast near Warden Point. A lighthouse marks the narrow opening into the Solent, and a signal-station signals outward and homeward-bound vessels to London.

To this lonely spot, on the 30th of November, 1648, was the captive king brought from Carrisbrooke Castle. Here he remained for a fortnight, till his final removal to London. His chamber is still shown,—such a mere cupboard of a room, that it can hardly have been more than one of his apartments.

Lymington has been a borough since 1150, but the earliest record of a mayor is dated 1319. It rose into note in the reign of Henry I., when it was made a port, and became celebrated for its salt-works, which extended along the coast to Hurst. In Edward I.'s reign, it contributed twice as many ships to the navy as Portsmouth. Gibbon, the historian, was at one time member for Lymington. But its salterns now are all closed, its oyster beds deserted, and its trade but a shadow of what it was. Yacht building and fitting, however, are carried out extensively. Inman's yacht yard is one of the principal.

Lymington lies on the right bank of the Boldre, or Lymington River, and consists principally of one long street sloping steeply to the river, with pleasant surroundings of villas and country houses. About a mile from the town are two camps, called Buckland's Castle, or Rings, supposed to be Roman. Outside the Needles, in Scratchell's Bay, " Samuel Baldrey, Esq., sojourner in this parish, was immersed 'sans cérémonie,'" in order, the story goes, that his wife might not dance over his grave, as she had often threatened.

An expedition, either by road or rail, to Boldre and Brockenhurst lands one in the heart of the New Forest.

Boldre is only one mile and a half from Lymington, and the church, omitting the village, can be reached by way of the Roman Camp at Buckland Rings, and across the stream by the bridge near the mill. It stands embosomed by oak trees, on rising ground, is mostly Norman, though it has been much restored. The battlemented tower was rebuilt in 1697. The churchyard contains some huge yews, and the views to the North and West are very fine. Gilpin, a former rector and a naturalist of note, author of "Forest Scenery," is buried here, and the quaint epitaph on himself and his wife should be noticed.

Brockenhurst, three miles farther on, is reached across the breezy, gorsy common of Setley, from which are fine views of the Isle of Wight in the distance. Brockenhurst, since the railway came to it, is being somewhat spoilt and be-villaed. It is an agricultural oasis in the midst of the Forest, but the straggling village is still beautiful. A deep Devonshire lane, shaded with old oaks, leads for a mile and a half to the ancient church, which is Saxon, 9th century, Norman, and Early English. It is the only church now within the forest, which is mentioned in Domesday, and stands on a hillock, its modern conical spire forming a landmark for miles, not unnecessary, probably, as a guide through the ocean of forest which surrounds it. The Norman door and font of black Purbeck marble, and the enormous yew, 18 feet in girth, in the church, should be noticed.

Brockenhurst Park (J. Morant, Esq.) is a fine place, with beautiful grounds. On the lawn are three large old oaks, probably the most ancient in the Forest. The grounds are opened on application, and the views thence are superb.

CHAPTER XV.

Up the Beaulieu River.

SAILING DIRECTIONS.—From Lymington follow the coast line with quite ½ mile berth. Make the Lepe Buoy, passing ¼ mile inside it. Get in one the two white beacons with black stripes on the hill, which will open the mouth of the river. This is beaconed both sides. Look out for a large boom on Bayonet Point close to entrance, where a tongue of mud runs out. Go up the river any time of tide, but if taken at half tide the channel is easier to see. Make the coastguard station at Needsor Point, and white building with tile top, but leave notice-board on starboard. Follow the channel up to Buckler's Hard, where you can lie afloat and row up to Beaulieu. Or go on to Speerhead Hole, not easy to find, and anchor in 10 feet.

At Lepe or Leepe, the entrance to the Beaulieu River, was the ford of Roman times alluded to in chapter viii., page 50. Here Henry II. landed to take the throne, and here Louis the Dauphin embarked after the battle of Lincoln. Inchmery, the yachting residence of Lord Delawarr, and Exebury House, among the trees, that of Mr. Forster, both face the river and the Solent. At Exebury Church is the grave of a former owner of the Manor House, William Mitford, the author of the "History of Greece.'

On the East bank is Bargery Farm, the old sheep farm of Beaulieu Abbey and S. Leonard's, now called the Abbey Walls, and which was their store farm. Here are ruined gable ends and other parts of an old barn, which must have been over 200 feet long. There are also ruins of a chapel. At Park, two miles to the East, was another chapel, now destroyed, close to the old farmhouse. Buckler's Hard is a quaint-looking spot to come upon in the midst of the wild and winding reaches of this woodland river, where the heron wings his heavy flight unmolested, and the wild swan sails out to meet the advancing yacht, and which is so rich in rare flora and wild life, owing to its sequestered situation. Buckler's Hard was laid out early in the last century as a town, for sugar-refining, by the then owner of the property, John, Duke of Montague, who was also the owner of S. Lucia, in the West Indies. But at the peace of 1748, that island being declared neutral, the Duke lost his property there, and the *raison d'être* of Buckler's Hard ceased. In the Napoleonic wars its importance revived, and it became a centre for ship-building, many large ships of war, even of 74 guns, being built there. Now the trade has entirely vanished, and a more desolate-looking place does not exist. The tony-looking houses of the last century are grouped round a green in a regular square, quite grass-grown. There is a general shop, where bread can be obtained. Nearer Beaulieu lies Bowvery Farm, the old ox-farm, or *bœuffré*, of the Abbey. A pleasant row it is up from Buckler's Hard to the wide mill pond at the head of the river. Reach after reach, with fine trees sweeping down to the water's edge, succeeds each other. It might be the upper Thames, only quiet, and undisturbed by traffic, and at the journey's end the great

Gate House of the Cistercian Abbey of Beaulieu rises among the old Wych elms.

In 1204, that wandering monarch of evil fame, King John, whose peregrinations up and down the coast, whose landings and whose embarkations we have so often noted in these pages, found himself at Lincoln. For some reason or other which tradition does not relate, he was much enraged with the Cistercians, and ordered all the abbots of the various foundations of that order to come before his presence. They obeyed, imagining to receive some favour, when, to their horror, the incensed king ordered that they should be trodden under foot by horses. The monks fled in terror, the soldiers hesitated for once to obey, and the king went to bed and dreamed a dream. He dreamt that he found himself at the last Judgment, where the ill-used abbots were directed to scourge him soundly. He awoke, still feeling the pains of the stripes on his back. Was it rheumatism? The fen country lies low. Anyhow the king sent for his director, and asked him, Pharaoh-like, what the dream might mean. The chaplain advised begging the monks' pardon, and conciliating an offended Deity by some munificence to his servants. The result was the foundation of Beaulieu Abbey, peopled by Cistercians from Citeaux, and endowed with lands in the New Forest and sundry exemptions. The Abbey was forty-two years a-building, and so lavish were the monks that it was 4,000 marks in debt when, in 1246, Henry III., with his Queen, his brother, the king of the Romans, and other notables, came to the dedication of the building. The stone had been brought from Binstead quarries in the Isle of Wight. Henry III., Pope Innocent, and Edward III., heaped gifts and privileges upon the foundation; the Pope granting the right of sanctuary, and the power to elect their own abbot, and the latter monarch a tun of wine to be delivered every Candlemas. Though the monks of Beaulieu were renowned always for their " hospitality, wealth, and piety," the foundation was swept away with the rest by Henry VIII. Through the Wriothesleys it has descended to the Buccleuchs and now to Baron Montagu, a younger branch of the latter house.

Beaulieu has been a place of refuge to more than one notable in English History. On Easter Day, 1471, was fought the battle of Barnet, when Warwick, the king-maker, was killed. That very day his wife, Anne Beauchamp, landed at Southampton, and learning the disaster, fled to Beaulieu. Here she was joined by Margaret of Anjou, who had landed at Weymouth with reinforcements, and fled to Beaulieu from Cerne Abbey, in Dorset, taking up her residence in the corner tower of the present palace, still called Queen Margaret's Tower. From Beaulieu the heroic Queen, accompanied by her son, marched across Dorset and Somerset to Tewkesbury, where was fought the battle which ended in the bloody murder of her son and her own imprisonment in the Tower. More than twenty years later the impostor, Perkin Warbeck, sneaked to Beaulieu, after deserting his allies at Exeter, was cajoled thence by fair promises, and met a traitor's death.

As one rounds the wooded reach which widens into the mill pond at Beaulieu, the Water Gate confronts us, leading to the Palace House, the Abbot's lodgings, rising among a wealth of fine trees, notably some Wych elms, silver firs and a hornbeam. Beyond the mill bridge, the mill head widens into an ornamental lake. To the left the village climbs the rising ground, and to the right beyond the Palace lies acres of the Abbey ruins. At the Dissolution the Palace was altered into a private residence, and was enclosed in a wall, and towers and moat were added in 1704 for fear of French privateers. The hall has a fine groined stone roof, and on the upper floor there is some good carving and a square decorated window.

The Abbey grounds, of which the walls can still be traced, extend over a square mile and a quarter. The church was equal in size to Winchester Cathedral, but only its foundations can be seen. A fine encaustic flooring has been excavated in several places, and protected by slabs of wood. A cross on the greensward marks the position of the high altar, before which was discovered the tomb of Isabella, wife of Richard, the king of the Romans, brother of Henry III., with her husband's heart in a marble vase beside her. The choir ended in an apse.

North of the church are the ruins of a winepress, from which brandy was certainly made less than 200 years ago from vines growing on the spot—a wonderful testimony to the mild and sheltered climate of this nook in the New Forest.

South of the site of the church are the ruins of the cloisters, with here and there a recessed seat. Three arches, once adorned with slender Purbeck shafts, are the entrance to the Chapter House. North of that again was the sacristy, and near it the Monks' Scriptorium. The dormitory is the best preserved of all the monastic buildings, having been used as a farmhouse. The kitchen and the sick-room, and the massive cellars, are fairly perfect, with fireplace, cupboard, and shelf, and are filled with masonry relics which have been dug up.

The refectory, a plain Early English building, was

transformed into the Parish Church, and is most interesting. The curious carvings on the bosses of the wagon-roof, restored recently in the same colours with which they were originally painted, should be noticed, especially a crowned head, supposed to represent Richard, king of the Romans; a woman's head-dress of the 13th century; and a crozier with the date 1204. The lancet windows are Early English, and the door at the North end (the church stands North and South) has splendid old iron scroll work. But the glory of the edifice is the beautiful stone pulpit, raised twelve feet up the West wall, the ancient rostrum of the monks. It is reached by stairs in the wall, with a double row of Purbeck columns supporting ribs and arches, and lighted by pointed windows with figures of SS. Bernard, Augustine, and Bishop Montague. The pulpit, which is demi-octagonal, projects from the wall. At each angle of the upper band are small sculptured buttresses, from the base of which a rib-moulding descends to a point, forming four triangles, the interior of each of which is richly carved. At Magdalene College, Oxford, there is a similar pulpit, almost as fine.

From Beaulieu to Hythe on Southampton Water (7 miles) the road lies across Beaulieu Heath, a heathery waste reached by a shady road to the Hill Top, with the Fir Garden of Scotch firs, planted in the last century by the Duke of Buccleuch, called John the Planter, who has left his mark in many places in the kingdom. Near here is the Monk Wells, whence water was taken to the Abbey, and which still supplies the village.

CHAPTER XVI.

Up Southampton Water.

SAILING DIRECTIONS.—Beaulieu to Calshot. Give the beach a fair berth off Stone Point, then get Calshot Spit Lightship (two masts), and Calshot Lightship (one mast), just open. Steer for "Black Jack," black and white chequered buoy off the Castle, passing inside latter lightship. Then steer for Castle, and anchor just inside in seven fathoms, and close by four fathoms. Land on gravel beach any time of tide.

To Hythe.—Steer for Fawley Buoy, in Fawley Creek Quay, then Cadland Beacon. Just above the beacon there is a private landing for Cadland House, and plenty of water to lie in the creek at any tide. Thence make two black and white buoys, and Hythe Pier. Anchor in a line with pier just below or above.

To Redbridge.—The river Test is buoyed up to Marchwood; beyond that beacons to Redbridge. Small craft can get up on any tide. At Marchwood there is a hard, and again at Crackenhouse Quay, Redbridge. Coming from Hythe, leave Southampton Pier on starboard, and the two buoys at end of The Gymp, on port side.

At Southampton.—Lie below the Town Pier, among the small vessels, or at the West Quay off the Royal Pier.

Up the Itchen.—Round the Light Vessel to Fairway Buoy on the Point. Thence the channel is beaconed to

Itchen Ferry. There are sixteen feet of water at L.W. Lie off Oswald's Yard, or by the vessels off Fay's Yard. At H.W. row up to Bitterne.

To Netley.—The channel is buoyed down to Netley. Anchor in mid-channel, close to Guardship, in three fathoms. Land at hard North of Government Pier, at the Pier, or at H.W. on beach.

Up the Hamble.—Buoyed all the way to the Hamble mouth, where is the last buoy, a red conical buoy, leave to port. The Hamble River is then beaconed all the way up to Bursledon Bridge. Leave the first two beacons on starboard. There is a hard at Warsash, and another at Hamble. Anchor just above Hamble on port side above the building yards, and above the hard. Small-class boats cannot get under Bursledon Bridge unless they unship their mast. Anchor there in mid-stream; nine feet water at L.W.

To Lee-on-the-Solent. — Coming out of the Hamble, steer for Baldhead Buoy. Then follow coast line, inside Calshot Light to Lee Pier, where you can land for a few hours except in West winds.

Titchfield River.—It is only possible to get in at H.W., and with local assistance, lying inside the haven, and rowing up at half tide. The beacon at the entrance has been washed down.

To Portsmouth.—If N. or E. winds, you can lie off Stokes Bay Pier, which make from Lee following line of bay. Then round Gilkicker Fort, allowing fair berth of 400 or 500 yards. If flood or half-tide, steer for Blockhouse, giving Haslar Hospital a fair berth. If L.W., steer through Swashway, getting the two marks on Southsea Beach in one, till you make the chequered buoy, then up Harbour.

The peninsula between the Beaulieu River and Southampton Water is almost entirely in the hands of a few large landowners, of whom Lord Montague and Mr. E. A. Drummond are the principal. It is highly preserved, and being remote from any railroad is comparatively inaccessible to the land tourist. Fawley, where there is a quay on a creek, is very pretty, the church most interesting, Norman and Early English. It is said to have been one of the four churches existing when the New Forest was made. A mile north is Cadland Park, Mr. E. A. Drummond's mansion, a finely wooded park. Eaglehurst, a quaint yachting residence belonging to the same owner, stands on the extreme point of the peninsula looking towards Cowes. It was originally called Luttrell's Folly, and is said to have been laid out by General Irnham, after the design of a camp of tents. Calshot Castle is one of Henry VIII.'s fortifications of the Solent, now only a coastguard station.

A run up the Test corner of Southampton Water will bring a reward in the shape of Eling Church, upon a spur of Eling Hill, overlooking the estuary, which, though much restored, contains Saxon and Norman work in flint and stone. At Redbridge, the head of the estuary, there is nothing to see, but it can be made a point for exploring the New Forest or a visit by train to Romsey Abbey.

Before the rise of Portsmouth, Southampton, even from the days of Canute downwards, was the great port of the Southern coast. It lies so well at the head of its great estuary, on a peninsula, between the rivers Itchen and Test. From Southampton sailed the armies that conquered at Crecy and at Agincourt. It was the great point of departure for France, the great port of call for the Venetian traders in the palmy days of the maritime

Republic. Hence sailed yearly also to Venice the "Flanders Fleet," so called. Southampton was plundered by the combined fleets of the French, Spaniards, and Genoese, and devastated by the Black Death later. Its importance declined, after Elizabeth's time, in proportion as that of Portsmouth rose. In this century it has returned. Steamship lines for nearly every part of the globe make it their headquarters; and though the P. and O. line have left it, the new American line make it their landing place, the Bremen line call there on their way to New York; and now that the new docks have been completed, the shipping trade of Southampton will undoubtedly go on increasing. In the eighteenth century it was the point whence fast sailing boats for the sum of five guineas would carry off runaway couples, to be united at Guernsey, where such marriages could be performed.

Approached from Winchester by an open common and an avenue, Southampton is a most interesting old town. At least a day can be well spent in exploring it. The town walls are traceable for a great distance, with their Norman towers, and especially fine are they on the West side. Part of the walls along the water's edge on the West side are carried on nineteen arches. Three gates exist: the Southern, Western, with groovings for three portcullises; these are Early Decorated. The northern or Bargate, Norman and 14th century, now inside the town, in the middle of the long High Street, which is distinguished as "Above Bar" and "Below Bar." The Guildhall is a spacious room over the Bar Gate, the north front of which is ornamented with gigantic figures representing the legendary hero of Southampton, Sir Bevis, and his giant Ascupart. The postern gate is to be seen near the arcaded piece of wall. The Water-gate at the end of the High Street, where it abuts on the quay, was taken down in 1804.

St. Michael's, Norman, and St. Lawrence's, Early English, are the two most interesting churches. God's House, Winkle Street, near the quay, was one of the earliest hospitals or almshouses founded in England, and dates from Henry III. It has been rebuilt, and is now used for French Protestant Service; but the chapel, dedicated to St. Julien, contains Transition Norman work. Here are buried the traitors, the Earl of Cambridge, Lord Scroop, and Sir Thomas Grey, who were beheaded at Southampton for treason in the reign of Henry V.

The antiquarian will find valuable specimens of ancient domestic architecture hidden away among the slums of old Southampton—in St. Michael's Square, in Simmel Street, in the Woollen Hall; in Blue Anchor Lane two, one with a Norman shaft in the chimney jamb. What is called the King's House, in Porter's Lane, should be noticed, *temp.* Henry II.

Near the South gate are twelve guns, mounted on a platform. One of them was recovered from the wreck of the *Rose Mary,* off Brading, in the reign of Henry VIII.

The Royal Southampton, the Royal Southern, and the Calshot Sailing Club for small-class yachts make their headquarters at Southampton. The first has a Club House Above Bar, the second on the town quay, and the third a new pretty little erection on the pier. Constantly during the summer there are races going in connection with one or other of the above in Southampton Water, the Calshot Sailing Club Races, with its little well-known " Southampton Flyers," attracting the attention of all yachtsmen, as their sporting little fleet skim down the great arm of the sea and round the " Brambles."

Within a walk of the town North, in Priory Road, are the scanty ruins of the Priory of St. Denys (founded 1124), with an inscription on one of the stones. Roman remains have been discovered at Bitterne, across the Itchen, the ancient Clausentium.

Southampton is a good point where to visit the New Forest by rail to Brockenhurst or Lyndhurst.

Passing down the East shore of Southampton Water, Netley Abbey must be visited.

Netley Abbey was a priory founded by Henry III. in 1237, and colonized by Cistercians from Beaulieu. Queen Elizabeth was entertained there by the Earl of Hertford, son of Protector Somerset. The Earl of Huntingdon turned the chapel into a tennis court, and the nave into a kitchen. Early in the 18th century it was bought by a Southampton builder, who intended to demolish it altogether. A dream, in which he saw that he was killed by the tower falling on him, dissuaded him from his purpose, but he met his death eventually by a stone falling on him from a window. In 1755 Walpole wrote enthusiastically of the sequestered and peaceful situation of Netley Abbey. Even thirty years ago it was quite remote and solitary. Now the ruins are trim and gardened under the auspices of the owner, Mr. Chamberlayne, of Cranbury Park, Winchester; the public are charged for admittance, and the new railway runs close by. The remains are, however, still extremely picturesque. They consist of the Gate-house, now called Netley Castle (Col. Hon. H. G. Crichton), fortified at the Dissolution; the outer walls of the church; the cloister-garth, or fountain court, from an old fountain in the middle, 114 feet square, and shaded with fine trees; the chapter-house, day-room, domestic offices, and the shell of the abbot's house, all Early English. A good view of the ruins can be obtained from the clerestory of the church, and there is a charming peep from the Abbey garden, east of the cloister court. Hound Church, Early English, was purchased from the monks by William of Wykeham.

The great modern attraction of Netley is the Military Hospital and Army Medical School, one of the many good works the nation owes to the late Prince Consort. It contains beds for 1,000 patients, as well as accommodation for military lunatics, and has a long frontage towards the river. The hospital is open to visitors. An obelisk commemorates the army medical officers who fell in the Crimea.

The Hamble is navigable for five miles up to Botley. But unless the mast can be shifted, Bursledon Bridge is the limit for sailing vessels.

Hamble was probably one of the earliest Saxon colonies in these parts. Up the wooded creek above Bursledon, near an ancient pier, was discovered in 1875, embedded in the mud, a Danish war-galley 130 feet long. Bursledon has some shipbuilding trade, but Hamble is the great centre for lobsters, a depôt for those brought round from the French, Irish, and Scotch coasts, and placed here in order to fatten for the London market. The church has been over-restored and spoilt; but that at Warsash, at the southern extremity of the river, is Norman and Perpendicular, with a rich Norman door.

Lee-on-the-Solent is a very new watering-place, with pier, but no particular attractions.

INDEX.

Agglestone, 66.
Alum Bay, 50, 57.
Alum Bay, sailing directions, 57.
Anchor, on getting away from, 4.

Ballard Down, 65, 66.
Barton Court Farm, 46.
Beaulieu Abbey, 87, 88, 89.
Beaulieu Church, 90.
Beaulieu River, 86.
Beaulieu River, sailing directions, 85.
Bedding for use on a yacht, 7.
Bembridge, 35, 36, 37.
Bembridge Harbour, 35.
Bembridge Harbour, sailing directions, 65.
Bitterne, 96.
Bitterne, sailing directions, 92.
Boar-hunt, 21.
Boldre, 83.
Bosham, 27, 28, 29, 30.
Bosham, sailing directions, 27.
Bournemouth, 80, 81.
Bournemouth, sailing directions, 80.
Boxgrove, 34.
Brading, 38.
Brading Harbour, 35, 36.
Branksea Island, 68, 69.
Branksea Island, sailing directions, 67.
Brockenhurst, 84.
Brockenhurst Park, 84.
Brooke, 55.
Buckler's Hard, 86.
Buckland's Rings, 83.
Bursledon, 97.
Bursledon Bridge, sailing directions, 92.

Cadland House, 93.
Cadland Creek, sailing directions, 91.
Calbourne, 52.
Calshot Point, sailing directions, 91.
Calshot Castle, 93.
Carrisbrooke Castle, 49.
Chichester Cathedral, 31, 32.
Chichester, 31, 32, 33.
Chichester Harbour, sailing directions, 31.
Chichester Bar, sailing directions, 24.
Christchurch Priory, 81, 82.
Christchurch, sailing directions, 80.
Cooking utensils, 9.
Cooking lamps, 9.
Cooking hints, 14.
Cooking for six days, 10, 11, 12, 13.
Corfe Castle, 75, 76, 77, 78.
Cowes, East Cowes Castle, 45.
Cowes, East, 45.
Cowes Castle, 47.
Cowes, 47, 48.
Cowes, sailing directions, 44.
Creech Barrow, 79.

Dockyard, Portsmouth, 17, 18.
Dull Quay, 31.

Eling, 93.
Emsworth, 26.
Emsworth Channel, sailing directions, 24.
Eucombe, 63.
Exebury, 85.

Fareham, 19.
Fareham, sailing directions, 18, 19.

INDEX.

Farringford, 54, 55.
Fog, what to do in a, 5.
Goathorn Point Hard, 68.
Godlingstone, 62.
Goodwood Park, 33.
Gurnard Bay, 50.
Halnaker Park, 34.
Hamstead, 52.
Hamble River, sailing directions, 92, 97.
Hamble, 97.
Hayling Island, 23.
Hayling Beech, sailing directions, 23.
Hurst Castle, 82, 83.
Hurst Castle, sailing directions, 82.
Hythe, sailing directions, 91.
Itchen River, 91.
King's Quay, 44.
Langston Harbour, sailing directions, 22.
Lee-on-the-Solent, 97.
Lee-on-the-Solent, sailing directions, 92.
Leepe, 85.
Lulworth Cove, 75.
Lulworth Castle, 75.
Lymington, 83.
Lymington, sailing directions, 82.
Main Bench, 59.
Medina River, sailing directions, 47.
Menu, a six days', 10, 11, 12, 13.
Moorings, on taking up, 4.
Mottistone, 52.
Necessaries, what, to take, 7, 8.
Needles, 58.
Needles Cave, 58.
Needles, sailing directions, 57.
Netley Abbey, 96.
Netley Hospital, 97.
Netley Castle, 96.
Netley, sailing directions, 92.

Newport, sailing directions, 47,
Newport, 48, 49.   [48.
Newtown, 51.
Newtown, sailing directions, 50.
Newtown Manor, 61.
Ningwood, 52.
Norris Castle, 45.
Nunwell Park, 38.
Old Harry Rocks, 65.
Osborne House, 44, 45.
Ower, 76.
Ower, sailing directions, 68.
Pilsey Island, 26.
Poole, 70, 71, 72.
Poole Harbour, 68.
Poole Harbour, sailing directions, 67, 68.
Porchester Castle, 20.
Porchester, sailing directions, 19, 20.
Portsmouth, 17, 18.
Portsmouth Harbour, 18.
Portsmouth Harbour, sailing directions, 16, 92.
Purbeck, sale of, 60, 61, 62.
Quarr House, 42.
Quarr Abbey, 42.
Recipes, cooking, 14, 15.
Redbridge, sailing directions, 91.
Redhorn Quay, 68.
Rivers, on tacking up, 5.
Roman Villa, 38.
Rue Street, 50.
Ryde, 42.
Ryde, sailing directions, 40.
Sailing Directions to—
 Alum Bay, 57.
 Beaulieu River, 85.
 Bembridge, 65.
 Bosham, 27.
 Bournemouth, 80.
 Bitterne, 92.
 Branksea, 67.
 Bursledon Bridge, 92.
 Cadland Creek, 91.

INDEX.

Sailing Directions to—
  Calshot Point, 91.
  Chichester Harbour, 31.
  Chichester Bar, 24.
  Christchurch, 80.
  Cowes, 44.
  Emsworth Channel, 24.
  Fareham, 18, 19.
  Hamble River, 92, 97.
  Hayling Beach, 23.
  Hurst Castle, 82.
  Hythe, 91.
  Itchen River, 91.
  Langston Harbour, 22.
  Lee-on-the-Solent, 92.
  Lymington, 82.
  Medina River, 47.
  Needles, 57.
  Netley, 92.
  Newport, 47, 48.
  Newtown, 50.
  Ower, 68.
  Poole, 67, 68.
  Porchester, 19, 20.
  Portsmouth Harbour, 16, 92.
  Redbridge, 91.
  Ryde, 40.
  Scratchell's Bay, 58.
  Seaview, 40.
  Southampton Water, 91.
  Southsea, 16.
  Studland, 64.
  Swanage, 60.
  Thorney Island, 24.
  Totland Bay, 57.
  Wareham, 68.
  Wootton, 40, 41.
  Wych, 68.
  Yarmouth, 53.
Scratchell's Bay, 55, 58.
Scratchell's Bay, sailing directions, 58.
Seaview, 41.
Seaview, sailing directions, 40.
Shalfleet, 52.
Southampton, 93, 94, 95.
Southampton Water, sailing directions, 91.
Southsea, 16.

Southwick, 21.
Squadron, Royal Yacht, 47.
St. Alban's Head, 62.
St. Denys' Priory, 96.
St. Helen's, 41.
Studland, 64, 65.
Studland, sailing directions, 64.
Swainston, 52.
Swanage, 60, 61.
Swanage, sailing directions, 60.

Tacking up rivers, 5.
Thorney Island, 24, 25.
Thorney Island, sailing directions, 23.
Tilly Whim, 63.
Titchfield, 19.
Tonnorbury, 23.
Totland Bay, 58.
Totland Bay, sailing directions, 57.

Utensils, cooking, etc., 74, 75.

"Victory," H.M.S., 17.

Warblington, 26.
Wareham, 73, 74.
Wareham, sailing directions, 68.
Warsash, 97.
Waterproof cover, 6.
Westover Manor, 52.
West Hampnett, 34.
Whippingham, 45, 46.
Whitecliff, 62.
Whitecliffe Bay, 37.
Wimborne Minster, 72, 73.
Wool, 74, 75.
Wootton, 43.
Wootton Creek, sailing directions, 40, 41.

Yacht, description of small, 6.
Yar, East, 35, 36, 39.
Yar, West, 53.
Yarmouth, 53, 54.
Yaverland Manor House, 37.

Lightning Source UK Ltd.
Milton Keynes UK
UKOW03f0850140314

228154UK00001B/35/P